"Joan Dornemann offers generous musical and emotional support to both professional and student singers. Her sensitivity to the singer's needs is unsurpassed." — **Renata Scotto**

"It is about time that Joan Dornemann wrote a book! It will take a book to get through even part of the wealth of information that she possesses through her wide experience." — **Mignon Dunn**, Mezzo-Soprano, Metropolitan Opera

"Joan Dornemann is the definitive opera coach in this country. She has the finest insight into the subliminal meanings of the text that go along with the way the composer has set it musically." — **Bradley Pennington**, Voice teacher, The Boston Conservatory

"Joan Dornemann works with singers in partnership, teaching them musical and emotional responsibility, something very rare today. She taught me that studying never stops. A coach of her caliber is voice teacher and coach in one." — **Barbara Daniels**, Soprano, Metropolitan Opera

"Joan Dornemann is one of the most outstanding coaches and teachers of operatic repertoire, acting and audition procedures. We have had great success with Joan Dornemann as a teacher here for a number of summers." — **Charles Webb**, Dean, School of Music, Indiana University

"Joan Dornemann continually challenges me to go beyond where I am as a singer and performer. She encourages me to explore myself in order to bring elements of a role to life." — **Gail Dobish**, Soprano, New York City Opera

"Sharing, caring, high art and expertise — these are what master-teacher Joan Dornemann is all about." — **Dr. Charles Kaufman**, Dean, The Mannes College of Music

"It has been my experience in knowing Joan Dornemann both personally and professionally that she is a wonderful musician, and an extraordinary human being with a great generosity of spirit. She has incredible knowledge developed through working in many opera houses and with great singers and conductors. She passes this knowledge on to singers in a gentle and efficient way. It is a joy to watch her in master classes." — **Marlena Malas**, Voice teacher, New York City

"At our institution, we have two categories of vocal students: 1) those who have been infused with the wisdom and warmth of Joan Dornemann's special art as a teacher and 2) the others. The difference is not a matter of taste, but a difference of insight, confidence and sheer accomplishment." — **Richard Adams**, Dean, Manhattan School of Music

"Joan Dornemann is a gifted teacher, offering a simple, direct approach to complex ideas. Her love for music and young singers is evident in her master classes." — **Stan Bartosiak**, Winner, Teacher of Teachers Award, Glendale, California

"Joan Dornemann changed my life." — **Raymond Sepe**, Tenor, Utrecht, Holland

From master class students:

"I look forward to the next master class. The last one was a shot in the arm in every way." — S.B.

"[Joan Dornemann] was able to zero in on problematic areas and not intimidate me." — J.P.

"I have already begun to implement your ideas and feel happy and energized to accomplish the goals I have set for myself." — L.W.

"After I worked with you, my teacher commented on how much and how well my voice was pouring out." — H.B.

Complete Preparation

A Guide to Auditioning for Opera

Joan Dornemann
with Maria Ciaccia

Introduction by
Sherrill & Nancy Milnes

Excalibur Publishing
New York

Published by:
Excalibur Publishing
434 Avenue of the Americas, Suite 790
New York, New York 10011

Cover design: Kara Glasgold, Griffin Design

Library of Congress Cataloging in Publication Data

Dornemann, Joan, date.
    Complete preparation : a guide to auditioning for opera / Joan
Dornemann with Maria Ciaccia ; introduction by Sherrill & Nancy
Milnes.
        p.   cm.
    Includes index.
    ISBN 0-9627226-3-4 (paperback)
    1. Singing—Auditions. 2. Opera companies—Auditions.
I. Ciaccia, Maria. II. Title
MT892.D67   1992
782.1'14—dc20   91-45883

Printed in the United States of America

1 2 3 4 5 6 7 8 9 10

For Marilyn and Eric

Table of Contents

Acknowledgments

A special acknowledgment to Carlos, Montserrat and Clarice, who believed in me first.

How does a coach learn? It's clear to me we learn from the singers, the stage directors and the conductors we work with. I have been more than fortunate in my life to work with the very best talent in the operatic world. I have had an incredible opportunity to learn from all these people. It is also a privilege to be part of the Metropolitan Opera, with its extraordinary standards of excellence, the joy of music and the comraderie among the artists. There is nowhere that we learn more than by being in the theater and by doing.

Maria Ciaccia is the only person I know with the ability to make my spoken words readable. I thank her for all her help in this project.

Joan Dornemann

I wish to acknowledge the following people for their invaluable help in the preparation of this book: Deborah Birnbaum, Ronnie Birnbaum, Myrna Paris, Kathleen Fogarty and Robert Trentham for their input; Alexis Greene for her detailed, patient and rich editing. A special thanks to Sharon Good for her support, wisdom and hard work.

A great deal of this book was compiled from tapes of actual master classes given by Joan. I would like to thank Jane Barthelemy and Cheryl Zrnic' for their class tapes.

Pamela Gilmore was a constant source of information and assistance. A mere "thank you" is not enough.

The involvement and generosity of Sherrill and Nancy Milnes was a wonderful and much-valued bonus in this project, and I shall forever be grateful.

A final thanks to Joan Dornemann for her magic. Nothing less could have given me back my love of opera.

Maria Ciaccia

Introduction

Joan Dornemann is without doubt the best known prompter/coach/auditions judge/master class giver in the operatic world. Nancy and I have known Joan for a long time and have taught with her, and worked and coached with her on many different roles over the years.

This book is long overdue in terms of need and value, because auditions, fortunately or unfortunately, are a sine qua non for careers. Although especially written for aspiring or current professionals, anyone singing on any level can learn much by applying the principles in this book. It presents practical advice for singers from the most naive to the most sophisticated, from the smallest town to the biggest city. Joan explores all the areas that a young singer needs for auditioning. Nancy and I especially like those particular phrases that deal with areas of singing that are not often discussed and are, in fact, very important in determining if one can have a career. For example: "[one must have] real ability with the necessary personality traits for a career," and "too many singers get lost along the way because of their personal inability to remain psychologically well-balanced while maintaining the difficult stance of being a student in the morning and a star at night."

Joan writes of specifics, of details, of the exact things to think about, the exact things to do, giving singers a thought process — not just to cross the fingers and hope that the voice will work well or that the arias chosen are accidentally right for that singer and for that occasion. Joan has her own way of presenting ideas, her own vocabulary and music. This way is very clear and concise, combining American savvy about music and singing with European traditions and style. She brings to mind musical moods we have all thought about, but never put into words. She gives the reader exact patterns to use to better communicate the emotion of a given aria or song. She also lays out practical work habits for all of us singers: how to study, how to review, how to use the mind more and the voice less. It takes more than a throat to have a career, and Joan Dornemann discusses it all.

Sherrill Milnes
Nancy Milnes
New York City, 1992

The secret of success in life: Prepare for
opportunity when it comes.

Benjamin Disraeli

Chapter One

Hurry Slowly

There is nothing more glorious than discovering the world of music and, more specifically, operatic music. All of us can remember when we first fell in love with opera. In my own case, my love of this art form led me from being a pianist to becoming a coach and prompter. I feel fortunate to be able to work with those who have voices able to communicate the beauty, warmth, passion and challenge of opera to an audience.

Unfortunately, in the world in which we live, an operatic voice can sometimes leave its possessor feeling frustrated rather than blessed. Dealing with the practicalities of life sometimes leaves us precious little time to pursue our art. The twenty-six or twenty-eight-year-old in any other field of endeavor is already climbing the corporate ladder; a singer is usually in the midst of intensive study. We may have to deal with friends and relatives saying, "When are you going to get a job?" There is an assumption that an opera singer cannot make a living. The career entry singer must often work as a word processor, receptionist or proofreader, for what seems like an endless period of time. What you *do* is those things; what you *are* is an opera singer.

But there is light on the horizon for the young singer. Once upon a time, there were one or two people who would perhaps help a singer or two. The beginner today has a much better chance. There are many more organizations, universities, apprentice and summer programs which afford opportunties for the young performer. The Metropolitan Opera, for example, helps thousands of singers, not only as an institution, through its auditions and Young Artists program, but through many of the singers with successful careers who take the time to help, advise and support young talent. For many years, teachers taught at the schools from which they graduated and never went far from home. A gifted teacher in that setting can give you only a certain kind of expertise. More and more, we have great performers who teach and are able to communicate a level of knowledge that is not only valuable to the young singer, but which saves him from time-consuming musical misadventures and serious career mistakes.

Another wonderful change is the explosion of opera in the media. You see opera performances and concerts on public television. Commercials use opera to sell products. Go to the movies and notice all the films that have woven opera into their plots.

But even with all of the increased interest in this country, there are still not always enough openings for all the wonderful singers we have, and opera companies suffer a chronic lack of funds. So the aspiring opera singer needs special equipment in order to survive the rigors and challenge of an operatic career — or more accurately, of *working toward* an operatic career. In comparison to getting the career, having a career may seem easy!

I'm aware that from where you are now, having a career doesn't seem easy at all. Strangely enough, we don't realize that there is lots of room at the top; it just might be a little hard to get through the bottom. Still, I have yet to see somebody with real ability and the necessary personality traits who couldn't climb the ladder.

The Importance of Mental Health

I believe one key is preparation, the preparation of your psyche as well as the music and voice. Given the necessary talent, of course, keeping on a healthy mental track is probably the straightest road to a successful singing career. Too many singers get lost along the way because of their inability to be psychologically well-balanced while attempting to maintain an unbalanced work life: being a humble student in the morning, able to take tons of criticism, and in the evening, a star worthy of an audience's rapt attention and a paycheck anywhere from $300 to $10,000. That kind of ego flexibility is not found in everyone. So it's one of the things for which you really have to plan and prepare. It's true, of course, that we all have to study; it's a privilege and challenge we enjoy our whole career. But being a *student* is a state of mind that we should enjoy for as long as appropriate and then move beyond. You can stop practicing to be students and start practicing to be professional singers — young, vital, focused, energetic, serious young professionals. Being a student is not the same as studying. The ongoing process of studying and learning, solving problems, discovering answers, finding new powers inside yourself, are some of the biggest thrills a performer can have.

Some of the best work done by the artists I know is done when they are slightly obsessive and self-involved. This is not surprising, since putting yourself on the line makes singers extraordinarily vulnerable, and preparation takes a great deal of commitment. After all, you carry your instrument in your body. It goes where you go. And the two small muscles in the throat that are your voice are not reliable in the same way as a Steinway piano is. As a singer, you not only have to build your instrument, but also learn how to play it, care for it and fix it.

I'm not saying you need to be obsessive (well, maybe a little). But you need to be someone whose mental health is kept up either by a very good support system or by an ability to be well-balanced and see that problems are often in the opera *business* and not within yourself.

So start to ask yourself some questions. Where is your support system? Where does it come from? What are your vulnerabilities? How can you be truly strong and not just propped up by the kind of flattery that is so dear to our hearts? How can you get to a point where you are supported by the real security of knowing your craft and knowing what it is you have to offer?

Your Career as a Business

To look on the practical side, you have to be prepared to deal with the business part of your life while working toward a career. What will you do when you come to New York to study, if that is your goal? Have you prepared yourself to work at a job while you're learning? Do you know how to fund-raise for yourself? Singing is expensive, and you can't afford to be casual or cavalier about your training. Fantasies and illusions about moving to New York and becoming a star overnight are enjoyable, but basically unrealistic.

There are some important basics to learn. Find out which people are informative — how to *network*, but not associate with people who are negative, non-supportive and gossipy. Learn the distinction between information and gossip. Learn it today. Information is something you can indulge in very freely, and gossip is something from which it would be best remove yourself. Almost everyone learns this the hard way. I found this out early in my career: I sat in a restaurant with a friend and gossiped about how awful our conductor was. We were astonished to learn later that his entire family and his manager had been sitting right behind us! Well, neither of us had those jobs very long. It had taken so much work to get that position, and I remember how quickly it was lost. You can make a habit of saying everything and anything *at home*. Tell your mother, your father, your sisters. Make it a rule that in your house you will say what you want to people who are related to you. But outside, do not indulge in the kind of thing that especially makes young people feel knowledgeable in this business: gossip and negative opinion.

Coping with Rejection

Opinion! Opinions make the discussion of opera and voices fascinating, and opinion has to be carefully distinguished from *fact*. If your coach says, "You're singing flat," this needs to be taken into account. If a manager says, "I don't think your voice is the right quality for the part," that's an opinion. Perhaps there is something in your voice that doesn't interest this person. While we don't feel terribly upset if we don't attract or interest every human being we meet, as singers, we can become very upset if every person in the musical world doesn't love our voice. It's truly a very vulnerable part of us.

It's important to evaluate the source of opinions and facts. However, you must realize that not everybody is going to like your voice. That doesn't make your voice bad. Think of the opera singers you don't like who have achieved great fame and are not at all bothered by the fact that you don't like them! Some voices, after all, are wonderfully controversial. But the truth is, as singers grow, they restudy and change some opinions and strengthen others. Successful singers (and I'm aware your definition of successful is someone who works all the time and doesn't have to sing in a restaurant) are still working on developing the perfect vocal technique. You can talk with most professional singers and hear long discussions on this subject. There really is no agreement in heaven. I thought everybody would *know* when I started working with the great singers.

Before setting out to audition, it's worth it to sit down and realize that if someone adores your voice, that doesn't make your voice great. And if someone doesn't adore your voice, that doesn't make your voice second rate. It can be hurtful, but rejection is part of this business. If you can't come to terms with rejection and learn to deal with it, the creative arts aren't for you! Of course, having a good attitude is helpful. It's so interesting to meet the singers who think that music was created just so their voices could be exposed to the public. Then there are those singers who believe, "Isn't it wonderful that I have a voice, because this music is so important and beautiful, I want to share it with everyone!" I think that's the attitude that supports you and helps you develop the most. Focus on developing your technique, so that you can be as creative as the music you love requires. Be ready to grow every day.

Know Yourself

Another key to coping with rejection is knowledge about the realities of your voice, knowledge about your present level, where you should be, where you are, your goals. Singing at the Metropolitan Opera is a lofty, exciting and compelling objective, but perhaps your first goal should be acceptance into the studio of the best voice teacher you can find. Then try to win a small competition, and eventually graduate to a bigger one. This can lead to working in a small opera company, obtaining management, moving on to a bigger company. It's all a process, a very exciting process.

Analyze yourself. How well do you take direction? How well do you remember? How flexible is your voice? How fast do you learn? How quickly can you deal with what a conductor wants, especially if it's different from what you've prepared? Those are skills that come from having security inside yourself. Security comes from the ability to deal with your instrument, from having a good technique and solid musical basics — good teaching, good coaching, good preparation.

Getting on the Right Road

I would love to get those of you young artists who are reading this book to the wonderful place where you have all the opportunities to perform that you want. Since that's not achievable in a book, I can hopefully get you started on the right road, the road to complete preparation. If you get nothing else from reading this, I would like you to begin to understand what *complete* preparation entails, and to share with me the great excitement and satisfaction that it can bring you.

I must acknowledge that the temptation for me to qualify nearly every statement in this book was almost overwhelming. Let me just state here that nothing is true one hundred percent of the time; everything is true some percent of the time. I can't pretend to bring everything to the depths that I would wish. Those depths can only be achieved between a teacher and a singer, a coach and a singer, in private, one-on-one sessions. This book will in no way replace those relationships; however, if you get just one idea that brings you further along, I will be happy.

The great singers of the past have left a wonderful operatic world, and it's up to us to take that world a step further. Each decade, there is more musical integrity, more dramatic involvement, more musical research and more operas to explore. There has never been a time when we needed singers more, to bring the world of opera into new dimensions and to preserve the kind of musical excellence that has grown in the last fifty years.

We have truly had great conductors and singers who have shown the utmost respect, love and joy for the study of the music itself.

Perhaps the most important rule I've learned in my lifetime, and one of the things that made a great difference in the way I studied, is an Italian phrase left to us by Toscanini: *il massimo di rigore, il massimo d'espressione*. That is, the combination of the maximum of correctness, exactness and excellence in study of the music and the maximum of expressiveness. To be merely correct is not enough. To be only expressive is not enough. It's the combination.

To take fear of exposure, to take self-doubt and limited experience and try to feel like you have the right to communicate something important on the stage is very hard. We all know that it's hard. But you have to do it, nonetheless.

I said to a teacher once, "Maestro, this is so difficult." He said, "Then, we'll do it difficult." The fact of the matter is, you have to do it anyway. I hear so many students say, "It's so difficult to really get into the character (or trill or sing low)." Well, difficult or easy, you have to find a way.

We can teach ourselves almost anything. We can teach ourselves to enjoy being on the stage instead of being terrified. We learn what we practice, and if we constantly concentrate on being nervous, we surely will be. If we practice in our minds and in our bodies and in our self-talk the idea that, "Oh, I can't wait till I get my chance to go out and perform," walking out onto the stage might seem like an opportunity rather than a barbaric penalty one has to pay for the desire to be a singer. (However, if after all this work, you find you're still a little nervous, that's okay. You can learn to work with it and turn it into an asset.)

In any case, walking out onto a stage, hopefully, is what you're going to be doing for the rest of your life. And the minute your foot hits the stage, you're "on." That may be hard to realize, because most singers wait until they start singing to be "on." It's important to build within yourself an idea that, yes, the stage is a place where I am *free* — to imagine, to live, to create, to be, to sweep the audience with me. Sometimes, because our upbringing tells us to be quiet and keep our hands still and voice low, it's hard to get up on stage and be an "exhibitionist." You don't have to rant and rave in life; you can still get up on stage and communicate whatever you want, be anything you want, as expansive and as charismatic as you can.

Preparation — The Key

One of the best ways to have a career is to be terrific. I'm serious. I asked a young singer in a class what people were going to like about his voice in ten years. The class laughed self-consciously when he said, "Beauty of tone." But that wasn't an egotistical statement. He thought it was the most important thing he had to offer. You each have something special. And if what you have is beauty of tone, work on the other things, but capitalize on that. Remember, we have three strong strands, like a braid to intertwine: voice, music and drama. Each one of these strands is important, and you may feel stronger in one area than the other. Enjoy your strengths, and work on building and developing your other strands.

While reading this book, keep in mind that a lot of great singers have broken the "rules": the weight rules, the range rules, the repertoire rules, the height rules, the age rules, and so on. Don't limit yourselves. Use this book to give you something to think about, to start you on your way. But never forget that your way is an individual one, and it's a path only you will walk to your particular destination. Learn from others, but retain your individuality. Be kind to yourselves, be patient and most important, keep your eye on the goal of sharing the glorious music you're gifted enough to be able to sing. Make your study and auditions fun and joyful. For the moment, they're your main performance opportunity.

Hurry slowly. Lesson number one.

⁂   ⁂   ⁂

Chapter Two

The Externals

"What difference does it make that I'm forty pounds overweight, if I sing great?"

Well, if you sing *great* it doesn't matter, in some theatres. If your voice is one of the wonders of the universe, if you've spent twenty years singing in the biggest opera houses in the world, if you're the only person in the world who sings a certain repertoire or knows a particularly obscure role, it probably doesn't matter. Remember what I said about breaking the rules? The director of a large opera company promised to pay a singer who was just starting out $500 a performance if she lost fifty pounds. Many years later, this now-famous singer said to me, "Now I weigh fifty pounds more, and they're paying me $5,000." But you have to sing great, great, great, great, great. If your voice is that phenomenal, close this book and relax.

For the rest of you, try to imagine that half your audience is deaf and the other half is blind. You, the opera singer, must reach both those who can only see and those who can only hear. Sometimes what we see *is* what we hear. People really do consider opera an audiovisual art.

Ask yourself — with so many excellent singers today and so much competition out there, why would you allow yourself any disadvantage, if it's a disadvantage you can control and turn into an advantage, or at least neutralize?

In a world where television/video is becoming a standard part of auditions and of opera, there's no way to avoid the fact that a singer's looks are important. Like it or not, externals count in audition and performance situations. It doesn't seem fair, and it isn't, but it is nonetheless so. And today, with so much social interaction in an opera company, the presentability of the singer as a person is important, offstage as well as on.

It's also true that what is suitable in a huge opera house is different from what is suitable in regional houses or in Europe. But in this book, I am dealing with the young singer who probably won't begin a career at La Scala, but does enter some competitions and apprenticeships, or sings in regional houses and perhaps does an audition tour in Europe.

The Importance of Choice

The hard thing to learn is, as you make your entrance in an audition, you can really be anything you want, as long as it's by choice. I *choose* to look like a poised, capable, experienced, dominating, strong person. I *choose* to look sweet and simple. Or I choose to look aloof or friendly.

I suppose it is possible for someone to wander out on stage having made no decisions as to what persona they wish to project, how they wish to dress, what repertoire they're really suited for, and be launched into an opera career, if they possess the voice of the century. But this book is not for the exceptions. Remember, you can be *exceptional*, and many of you reading this probably are, and, unfortunately, still have a very *ordinary* career course. If something marvelous happens to pluck you from obscurity the second you leave college, great! But if not, be ready to work, to prepare, to choose.

The definite no-no is the person who comes out on stage to sing looking like he or she really hates being there, hates singing, hates the procedure and wishes he or she had never seen the audience or heard the music. Anything else is forgivable — even making a mistake in the music. Suppose you forget the words, blow a line, crack on a note? It's possible, and heaven knows, it's happened to a thousand professional singers. So you're not perfect. But being afraid to allow your personality to glow, to be a part of the music, is not a good choice. We don't want to hire stone statues for opera.

Make sure that everything you wear or carry on stage is the result of a choice. No young person chooses with the experience of an older person, but the one advantage you have over an older, more experienced singer is your youth and your enthusiasm in auditioning for the first time. Deal with yourself and with your externals at an appropriate professional level. The kind of person who wanders out on stage not knowing what they're doing there doesn't make a good impression on their listeners. It's also not living up to your responsibilities as an artist.

Your Strong Points

Making the most of your strong points is probably one of the most important things a young singer can do, and seldom does. If you don't know how, you can ask people who can help you. There are books on clothes, on make-up and on make-overs. Use everything you need. Call your friends. Hire an expert. Remember, it is most important that the dress enhance the person, but not upstage you or the audition. It's like building a house in a natural setting — both the landscape and the house must be enhanced. Some singers put on a dress or a suit that's so terrific, it's all you see. Or the dress or suit is wonderful, but just doesn't belong on that person.

It doesn't matter if you're dressed like the character you are auditioning for or not, as long as you're dressed in a way that looks as if you belong in a theater, not a kitchen or a gym. Auditioners can always see quality and care. We understand if somebody can't afford to shop in high-fashion stores, and that really doesn't matter, but thought, planning and choosing are all important.

Someone in your local dance studio, or an exercise teacher, can give advice about your walking and movement. It does seem like a long way from the edge of the stage to the piano, and there are an infinite number of ways to get there. Your entrance can have purpose, impact and look as though there is an affinity between the stage and you. (You also don't want to fall down!)

There's nothing like having a videotape made of yourself and, after about a week of terror, sitting down, perhaps with your teacher or a good friend, to really look at it *analytically*. You will find that a videotape shows you a great many things you do *well*. It shows that you don't look like a stone statue or that you are not constantly in motion. But it also may show that your walk or posture could be better, that your facial expression as you announce your name and your pieces could be more poised, your voice clearer, faster, slower, warmer. If you're in a situation where you don't have many teachers, at least the bimonthly use of a videotape gives a good record of your progress, gives you more confidence and shows the places that need work.

Women, you can always go to an expensive department store (but leave all your credit cards at home). Go with someone whose taste you respect. Try things on. Get an idea of the right style for you. Then head for the inexpensive districts and see if you can find a reasonable facsimile or have one made. Ask yourself, What is the image I want to project? Diva-ish? Pert? Sexy? Innocent? If possible, check the color of the curtain you'll be singing in front of, so you don't wear a dress that fades into the background because it's the same color. Keep your hair styled. If you need help with your make-up, get it.

Men, polish your shoes! Use shoe trees so the ends of your shoes don't curl. Make sure you shave (or trim your beard). No wrinkles in the suit. A shirt with a comfortable collar that allows you to sing. These sound like nonsensical details, but they are important ones. And these are details that, in preparing one's voice and getting to an audition, are sometimes forgotten — and often noticed by auditioners. Even if they're not noticed, attention to detail will make you feel cared for, special, polished and prepared.

The Weight Controversy

Back to the weight question. We all wish we were five pounds thinner, but if you're talking about fifty, get at it *before* you audition. Obviously, opinion about weight ranges may differ for a light lyric or a dramatic soprano, but you don't have to be overweight to sing, and you don't have to be overweight to have a big voice. Understand your build and your voice type and be realistic about your weight. It's not necessary to be a perfect size eight. Being thin-thin is not required. I am talking about an appropriate size for the role and the house where the opera is being performed.

Most regional houses want a package, a total of sound, style and look. Unless you have the fabulous gifts of Joan Sutherland, it will be difficult to be hired for *Fille du Regiment* or *La Traviata* if you're oversized. The days of the extra large Mimis are coming to an end. I've chosen examples of women's voice types and roles, but, of course, the same is true for men. Excess weight will work against the aspiring Duke or Alfredo just as it will against the would-be Gilda or Violetta.

Externals really count. Remember, when you walk out on stage, we see you before we hear you. You haven't started to sing yet. Don't be counted out before you do.

%   %   %

Chapter Three

Repertoire

Now let's talk about when you do start to sing. What *are* you going to sing?

It's helpful to take a long look at the total distance you will want to go in your career. It's one thing when you're twenty to say, "If my career only lasts twenty years, it's okay." But young singers don't realize how soon forty comes and how much you may not want to give up singing at forty.

Try this. Write down your age and what you're singing now. Then write down what you see yourself singing in five years. Ten years. Fifteen years. Twenty years. Is there a progression there? If you are singing Wagner today and you're twenty-five years old, what are you going to be singing when you're fifty? If you aspire to be an Aida at forty and you're twenty-six now, you should perhaps be looking at Donizetti, Mozart, lyric Verdi now and let yourself grow into that more demanding repertoire. There should be reasonable room for growth and change. And if you're going to make a mistake, make one that will help you live a longer vocal life, not a shorter one.

Let's pretend that voices come in sizes, like gloves and shoes. I find the most common mistake is that a young voice, which is probably a size five or six or seven, goes into auditions singing size ten, eleven or twelve music. It's fun to try out the heavier repertoire occasionally, so if you're a lovely, light lyric soprano and you feel like it, sing Butterfly for twenty minutes one day, once! If you're twenty-two and you want to sing all those wonderful arias from *Aida* and *Il Trovatore*, go ahead and sing them once a year.

But the best way for you to grow in your repertoire is the way music itself grew. It started with Handel, Monteverdi, Pergolesi, Donizetti, Bellini and Rossini. That's where you can start, too. Richard Strauss and Wagner came much later in the musical scheme. In your little schematic of what you should sing when, perhaps that later repertoire should come when your skills and your voice are really developed and formed.

When you look at the singers who are smart, you see that Mirella Freni, as an example, began by singing Adina, later moved into some of the Verdi/Puccini repertoire and is only now singing *Manon Lescaut* and *Il Trovatore*. She's still singing great.

The Proper Repertoire

For some reason, everyone wants to be three fachs bigger than they are. Perhaps part of this comes from the misconception that auditioners only want to hear big voices. The fact is, a beautifully resonant, well-projected voice of quality, expression and style is more important than size.

Size is a very misunderstood word in relation to voices. Opera singing is probably the only time when everybody thinks the best thing to do is to be big. The projection of your voice does matter. The size of your voice doesn't really matter, as long as you're in your appropriate repertoire. Your goal is ultimately to perform in a theater with an orchestra, so ask yourself, Who's going to sing Susanna and Don Ottavio if all we have are sopranos for *Aida* and tenors for *Turandot?*

Some singers feel that if they are too heavy physically — if they are, say, a Mimi in Brunhilde's body — that singing heavier repertoire will help them get roles. It generally doesn't work.

Another common misconception comes from the singer in an "overpopulated" fach, for instance, the lyric soprano fach — Marguerite, Micaela — who feels that because there is so much competition for these roles, the solution is to move into Tosca and Salome. Wrong. The solution is to make what you do so special in your right repertoire that you will be hired.

Recently, a friend of mine from the Metropolitan Opera telephoned to tell me of a great opportunity. She said a singer was needed to do a fantastic concert in Europe of Rossini arias. I thought to myself, Who is ready? Who has their pieces ready? I could think of only two people who were really prepared to perform a Rossini aria. And yet, there is a Rossini aria to fit almost everybody. When you begin to understand that the programs, the concerts, the operas themselves can't be put on without the singers, you begin to understand why sometimes the American singers, with all their great superiority of technique, sometimes lose out to European singers, who concentrate more on readying what is *appropriate*. Perhaps they are more practical in their approach.

Too Much, Too Soon

When a young singer goes into an audition and announces she is going to sing "Pace, pace" from *La Forza del Destino*, or he is going to sing King Philip's Monologue from *Don Carlo*, the reaction is almost always, "Why have you chosen this?" If you intend to sing the most difficult arias in the repertoire for audition, be sure it's an appropriate choice for you and that you're up to the challenge.

Those big arias are also full of little mysteries. There's a wonderful line from a Mario Lanza film, "These arias don't give up their secrets easily." The young singer hasn't been studying long enough to flesh out these arias. For that reason, these pieces can serve you poorly. In auditions, sing arias that add to you right now, not ones that point up what you don't have yet.

And before you embark upon learning these huge arias, please bear one other thing in mind. Muscle memory is a very powerful thing. It's hard to change a physical habit (think what it would be like if you had to learn to walk another way). If you learn these pieces when you're young and not at the height of your vocal maturity, re-learning them later in life can be a difficult, frustrating and expensive process. So don't learn every famous aria in the anthology — please, I beg you. Otherwise, you're going to spend a lot of time undoing the mistakes in order to relearn the aria.

Naturally, if you are older, performing the more dramatic repertoire can be much more appropriate. First of all, the voice is mature enough to do so, and second, you usually have a stronger and more defined vocal technique, plus some stage experience to help you cope with keeping your voice in good shape while you are singing music with a high degree of emotional impact. Each singer is a very special case and must be dealt with on an individual basis. This approach sometimes can result in having a wonderful, if short, career.

You have heard that the opera houses in Europe are small so that it's easier to sing a heavier repertoire, but you can find yourself in a European house that is not very good acoustically, so it doesn't always make a difference that they're smaller.

Going out and tackling your biggest, hardest aria doesn't necessarily win you any extra points. Strangely enough, I've seen competitions won by people who sang pieces that weren't very "showy." "O mio babbino caro" from *Gianni Schicchi* or "Steal me, sweet thief" from *The Old Maid and the Thief* — uncomplicated, not long, but when extraordinarily well-sung by a well-balanced voice and beautifully prepared can be real winners. You do want to show all the aspects of your voice, to demonstrate all your special abilities of range, color and technique. Those are the qualities that count, not only the difficulty of the piece. It's better to have too much — too much richness in your voice and a lengthy career are better than reading in the paper, "Not quite up to the role of . . ." That sort of thing is so easily avoided if one is judicious in choice of repertoire.

Having five arias that show your vocal and artistic range and are beautifully prepared means that you go into an audition feeling great. You have ten minutes to give them a lot of information about your voice. And since we acknowledge that very few singers are perfect, auditioners will also hear the imperfections. This is normal, and there really is nothing to fear.

Be miserly in your repertoire, so that you can give it the preparation and attention it deserves. Repertoire is important; it's important to your longevity as a singer and to your vocal health, growth and artistic success.

Choosing Repertoire

Repertoire for study is one thing; repertoire for performance is another; repertoire to help your voice learn how to do certain things, your study pieces, is still another. Ask yourself what you're learning from the piece you're singing. If you're not getting musical, dramatic or vocal knowledge out of the piece, perhaps you shouldn't sing it yet.

The song repertoire should definitely be part of your study repertoire. When preparing your music, remember, there are all kinds of auditions that are important: auditioning for a voice teacher or a coach, auditioning for a competition, auditioning to get one step higher on a rung. You don't always have to sing an aria to do it. Don't neglect the song repertoire. For instance, learning every Verdi song before you learn every aria can teach you a lot about the style. Otherwise, it's like trying to learn to pour cement at the most crucial moment in housebuilding. The arias can come a little later.

All those Italian songs certainly sound impressive and beautiful when sung by Luciano Pavarotti. And I'll bet you don't even want to look at them again. Can you really do without these songs that are so good for the voice? Can you do a three-second crescendo and a three-second diminuendo on the beginning of "Caro mio ben," and can you get your voice even with no bumps? How many of you can do a very fine half step and whole step trill yet? What about messa di voce? Scales, thirds, ups and downs, staccatos, jumps, portamento?

In the long run, in spite or because of everything your teachers and coaches do, you teach yourselves. You have to find your best sound. I know you want to sing all the great operatic music, but you need good technical grounding. The song repertoire can certainly help you achieve that; the Italian song repertoire of Bellini, Donizetti, Verdi, Tosti, Rossini, Respighi, Pizzetti, are all too often neglected, but are excellent to work on.

Almost every young voice is a lyric *something*, which is important to remember in your choice of repertoire. Also, just because your voice is right for a certain aria doesn't mean you're ready to sing the entire role. Entire roles require a level of stamina and maturity not usually found in very young voices.

Repertoire for audition has to include a piece that works for you, a piece that gets to that gravitational center of your voice soon. Where is the bulk of the beauty in your voice? And does this piece get there soon? It's like a woman's make-up. Do your make-up and dress draw us to your eyes? Or your hips? Which do you want us to look at?

If you have a terrific E natural, "Quando m'en vo" from *La Bohème* can be an excellent beginning piece. If you need a longer time to warm up, maybe the recitative from Micaela's aria from *Carmen* is a better beginning. The combination of pieces that you're going to use is a very big part of your repertoire preparation in several ways. Maybe the low notes in "Ah! non credea mirarte" from *La Sonnambula* work better if you sing it before "The Bell Song" from *Lakmé*, for instance.

Your audition list works best if it informs your listeners instead of confusing them. Sing the repertoire you do well, and perhaps add in one aria that gives an indication of what you think you will grow into. The good-sized lyric soprano might list Micaela's aria, "Mi chiamano Mimi" from *La Bohème*, the "Jewel Song" from *Faust*, and quite possibly "Tacea la notte" from *Il Trovatore*. This is my present; that is my future.

This not only applies to opera, but to oratorio and lieder as well. You ought to be prepared in all types of music — prepared musically, vocally, dramatically and linguistically — and have each component at the highest possible level.

Let's go through some voice types and some *conceivable* repertoire, but before doing so, I want to emphasize that these arias are just *examples*. Even within vocal categories, repertoire differs slightly from singer to singer. Also, no singer chooses repertoire in a vacuum. You will be doing so with the help of informed teachers and coaches. And as you mature, sometimes even over a period of a few years, as more of your voice is excavated, some of your repertoire will develop and change. What I hope to do with the following examples is to help you become attuned to a discernment process and start you on the road to understanding your own voice and your own progression. There are lots of good arias for you to look at in the new anthologies.

Check into them! An interesting source of arias is Tom Grubb's book, *Singing in French*. It has a list of arias for each voice type that is very comprehensive (this book is also wonderful for your French diction).

The Tenor

Lyric tenors. Let's say right now you're singing *Lucia di Lammermoor* and *L'Elisir d'Amore*. Perhaps you have the range and flexibility to do *L'Italiani in Algieri* and some coloratura, as in the Don Ottavio role in *Don Giovanni*. But you feel as though your voice is going to develop into more *Rigoletto*, more *Les Contes d'Hoffmann*, more *La Bohème*. If you're twenty-seven now, by thirty-two, it's not inconceivable that you might be growing into that repertoire, and you might want to add a fuller piece at the end of an audition list to indicate this.

A tenor may be singing *Gianni Schicchi* now. In five years, he may add *La Traviata*, and five years later, perhaps *La Bohème* and *Madama Butterfly*. In that situation, it can be helpful to take a Verdi piece that is somewhat full, like the aria from *Macbeth* — not a really killing tenor role, but a small role with a nice dramatic piece — so that you're not doing *Aida* yet, but you are doing a full Verdi aria without assuming the responsibility and difficulty of a full Verdi opera.

For the weightier lyric tenor, *Carmen* is nice for switching between lyric tenor and not-so-lyric tenor, as is *La Favorita*. The tenor role in *La Favorita* really progresses from lyric to heavier lyric. An aria like "Pourquoi me reveiller" from *Werther* is sung by both lyric and dramatic tenors, such as Franco Corelli and Nicolai Gedda. The roles of Faust and Edgardo in *Lucia di Lammermoor* are roles that tend to stay well in the voice as the voice grows; they're not unheard of for the lyric tenor. The first act of *Faust* is a little heavy, but this is preferable to Don José in

Carmen. Yes, José begins lyrically, but it becomes very dramatic. The title role in *Ernani*, as another example, is a lyric tenor role that includes a very difficult dramatic aria, one which perhaps is not so easily done without a really developed technique.

Alfredo in *La Traviata* is a role often picked by young students, although *Traviata* is a challenging opera to sing in tune and to bring out the essence of the character for the tenor. However, Alfredo is an excellent opportunity role, as is Pinkerton in *Madama Butterfly*. Pinkerton is a heavier role because of the orchestration — you really need to be able to get over the orchestra. On the other hand, there are only two acts. If you're going to choose something that might be beyond you, better something with two acts than four. So if it's between a really heavy *Tosca* and a *Madama Butterfly*, maybe *Madama Butterfly* is better to start with.

Ah, you say, if you're talking about short operas, what about Turiddu in *Cavallerìa Rusticana*? True, Turiddu is also not long. However, it has a large, intense emotional range — it's not the same type of role as Otello, certainly, but it is an extraordinarily tense, dramatic role that can unleash the voice into perhaps unwarranted emotionalism for a young singer.

Sometimes, if a singer has a really lyric voice, he or she is advised to sing Mozart. But the tessitura of Mozart can be really beyond your vocal staying power at a young age. I have found Mozart to be wonderful for the voice, but sometimes just too much, too hard. Too clean a line is required, more than a young singer's technical facility can handle. Also, in the young singer, there can be a *misunderstanding* of the style required for Mozart. The inexperienced singer may hold in his or her voice in an unhealthy way, attempting a delicate approach, inhibiting rather than opening the voice. For instance, "Ich baue ganz" from *Die Entführung aus dem Serail* is a good piece to study for the voice, but the tessitura might not be comfortable, in which case, wait a little while. "Se il mio nome," the serenade from *Il Barbiere di Siviglia*, is comfortable for everybody. *L'Elisir d'Amore* is also wonderful to work on. *Manon*, with its good combination of lyric-dramatic is really better to study than the Italian *Manon Lescaut*, which requires a more dramatic approach. *Roberto Devereux* calls for a higher tessitura, intense drama and lyric singing. Any one of these operas mentioned can take the lyric through spinto.

Some tenors are well advised to look at comprimario roles, because they have the acting, musical and vocal abilities suited to these important roles. For the young man who hoped to sing Rodolfo, this might require some extra thought and planning. But every opera needs the participation of this most important voice type.

The Baritone

For the lyric baritone, there is *Don Pasquale*, *Il Barbiere di Siviglia*, *Die Zauberflöte*, *Il Matrimonio Segreto* and the smaller roles in the bigger operas. Utilize the French repertoire — *not* Escamillo in *Carmen*, but perhaps something like Albert in *Werther*. The Count in *Le Nozze di Figaro* is one of the tricky ones. It is not dramatic; on the other hand, it is also not high. The same is true of Ford in *Falstaff*, which is not particularly dramatic but requires drama in the voice. This music needs to be well thought out to be used. Operas like *L'Incoronazione di Poppea* and *Faust* contain classic lyric baritone roles that can be sung from more lyric to more dramatic within themselves. You might want to practice, just for singing's sake, the Macbeth aria and *Don Carlo*, to work on good legato and good expression. But consider the tessitura of your voice and the tessitura of the piece. Sometimes the lyric voices do not yet have high notes that are easily accessible, in which case, something like *L'Elisir D'Amore* is wonderful. True, *Elisir* is not a dramatic piece; on the other hand, it doesn't have fourteen high G's.

Much of the Donizetti and Bellini repertoire is dramatic in its concept, but not in weight. Silvio in *I Pagliacci* is just as "dramatic" as Tonio in the same opera, but the *weight* of the voice is entirely different. Until those dramatic qualities begin to settle into the voice and personality, there are many superb operas in the early Italian repertoire, such as *L'Italiani in Algieri*.

The Bass

Basses have an enormous flexibility of repertoire — not a lot of starring roles, but very many big ones. Those are very good ways to get yourself out onto the opera stage. Mozart has given basses magnificent roles such as Sarastro in *Die Zauberflöte* and The Commendatore in *Don Giovanni*. Osmin in *Die Entführung aus dem Serail* is a good bass role for the singer with a strong middle range and good low notes. Basilio in *Il Barbiere di Siviglia* is an excellent singing and acting role. Many bass roles are not overly demanding; Zuniga in *Carmen*, for example, is an important role, but not lengthy one. Later, Boris Godunov is a great role the bass can look forward to.

Many bass *buffo* parts are sung by older baritones, and on occasion, they're not really sung at all, but rather, carried with the enormous weight of the singer's personality. I am not sure that this was intended by the composers, but it is effective. These roles have a very special tessitura, usually high. But if you really sing them with good technique, a healthy voice and a good stage presence, these can be marvelous, profitable roles. In fact, there are so many operas that we don't do much today, because this kind of bass with the proper vocal and acting ability is so hard to find (*Il Matrimonio Segreto* is one of those operas).

The Soprano

For the lyric soprano: *Les Pêcheurs de Perles*, for the lyric with agility, as opposed to Micaela, which is lyric without requiring agility. *Romeo et Juliette* is also lyric as far as the actual opera is concerned, but the aria has a higher extension and more flexibility. It's a nice place to start. *Lakmé* is lyric, with fiendish coloratura for the aria.

Adina in *L'Elisir D'Amore* is a great place to begin for the lyric soprano, as is Susanna in *Le Nozze di Figaro*. These roles allow the voice full range and do not suffocate it. They also don't have the cruel tessitura and the big high notes of *Lucia di Lammermoor* or *I Puritani*. For the young lyric, Lauretta in *Gianni Schicchi* is good for the voice. Much depends on the center of the voice and the flexibility, not to mention the color. Is it a brilliant or a dulcet color? Is there a plangent feeling to the sound? Or is it an exciting, edgy brilliance? Pamina, for instance, requires a special color and helps work on pianos and legato.

Micaela in *Carmen*, Manon in the French *Manon* and Marguerite in *Faust* are lyric roles which become a bit more dramatic. As the voice takes on more presence, with a really good A natural and high C, Mimi in *La Bohème* can be added.

Butterfly, while it may look easier than some big lyric roles, has a lot of wear, just for sheer on-stage time. And *I Pagliacci*, while it is short, is extremely intense. But *I Pagliacci* can be a good transition to a heavier repertoire, as can Margherite in Boito's *Mefistofele*.

Once in a heavier repertoire, look first at roles like Elvira in *Ernani*, Leonora in *Il Trovatore* and Violetta in *La Traviata*. These are all Verdi roles that require a rich sound with lots of flexibility. Violetta, in particular, demands a special dramatic presence and grace. Aida, Leonora in *La Forza del Destino* and Amelia in *Un Ballo in Maschera* come later. At that point, you have to be very sure of the strength and tenacity of your technique and the maturity of your voice. The many Mozart heroines — Elvira and Donna Anna in *Don Giovanni*, Fiordiligi in *Così Fan Tutte*, Elektra in *Idomeneo* — provide exciting vocal adventures for the soprano.

The Mezzo-Soprano

Like sopranos, mezzo-sopranos come in many types: lyric, lyric coloratura, dramatic and dramatic coloratura. For lyrics, Cherubino in *Le Nozze di Figaro*, Octavian in *Der Rosenkavalier*, and Charlotte in *Werther* can be looked at. The lyric coloratura finds excellent repertoire in Rossini's heroines: Rosina in *Il Barbiere di Siviglia* and the title role in *La Cenerentola*. The Rossini tragic operas are suitable for the dramatic coloratura: *Semiramide* and *Tancredi*. The pants roles are very interesting: the Page in *Romeo et Juliette*, Smeton in *Roberto Devereux*, and many more.

If the tessitura of the voice lies generally high, then the bel canto repertoire is much more suitable, such as *Roberto Devereux* and *Norma* — bel canto operas that require flexibility, but not the same coloratura that is needed in *Il Barbiere di Siviglia*. If your voice is rather dramatic, then you need the slightly heavier bel canto pieces.

For the dramatic mezzo, there is Azucena in *Il Trovatore*, Amneris in *Aida* and the Wagner mezzo roles. Again, I urge you to look at these roles when your voice has achieved a certain level of maturity. The great mezzo Christa Ludwig began with Cherubino, the Composer and Octavian, then attacked Amneris and the Wagner and Strauss roles! Fiorenza Cossotto's early career encompassed Adalgesa and Suzuki, then Azucena and Amneris.

The more dramatic mezzo often chooses to audition with "O don fatale," Eboli's grand aria from *Don Carlo*. It is true that this aria is a great selling piece, but it's such an advanced piece of opera (and also has the distinctive problem of having been written in French and rewritten in Italian) that it's a difficult aria to work on. Most of *La Favorita* is wonderful; however, the aria is treacherous because it passes in and out of what some people call "breaks." It will either help train you or show up your difficulty. But the rest of the opera is great.

The "In-Between Voice"

There are different kinds of casting that go on all the time. Zerlina in *Don Giovanni* is often a cross-over, done by both mezzos and sopranos. The best way to answer a casting question is to figure out where your voice works. Where is the center of gravity in your voice? Work in the tessitura of your voice that's accessible — for *Le Troyens, Pelléas et Mélisande* and *L'Incoronazione di Poppea*, you can be a mezzo or soprano. Carmen has been sung by sopranos and mezzos; Cherubino is at times sung by lyric sopranos.

There is the often disconcerting, but exciting process of a young mezzo whose voice is decidedly going up. These singers must learn to accept nature's decision and enjoy the process. If you're switching from mezzo to soprano, Musetta in *La Bohème* can be very helpful, as can the Desdemona aria, bringing you into the soprano world little by little. "L'Altra Notte" from *Mefistofele* is also helpful in carrying over your training.

There are even those medium baritone roles for the person who is caught between tenor and baritone and who is not sure whether he's going up or down. Pelléas, if you're a superb musician and have a gift for French, can be a role for the person in between, as well as Eisenstein in *Die Fledermaus*, Danilo in *The Merry Widow* and Nerone in *L'Incoronazione di Poppea*. Those are four roles for somebody not sure where their voice is, a common problem for younger baritones.

Yes, it's important to sound like what you are, but not too early. You might not know before age twenty-seven what your voice wants to be. Do not impose. Let your voice go where it wants. Be a good teacher and a good parent and a good trainer. Your voice sometimes doesn't start off where it's going to end up. This is not a crime against nature. Wasn't Mr. Bergonzi a baritone, and wasn't Ms. Scotto a mezzo-soprano? Juan Pons was a bass. This is the result of a voice's taking away certain things that it finds it doesn't need to do, and like the wonderful helium balloon, up it goes. Or in some cases, down it goes. The idea is to follow your voice, be flexible. And it's often the case that someone has the soul of an Italian, but their voice cries out to sing German. There's no reason why the voice shouldn't have its way.

What You Do Best

"But everybody tells me a different thing" is a common problem. Don't worry (if you can help it). As your voice takes on more personality, more assurance, it will settle down into what it does best. But in the beginning, it's rather changeable and, of course, frustrating.

Vocal category is not a reflection of your worth as a person. You won't be a better person if you're a tenor. You won't be a better person if you're a mezzo-soprano; you'll just work less, if you are really a soprano trying to be a mezzo-soprano.

Ask yourself what kind of personality you could play on the stage. Are you a Don Giovanni or a Leporello? Some singers have to look for a long time to find repertoire in which they are marketable; it's like trying on clothes. However, once they find that repertoire and make a name for themselves, it seems there's nothing they *can't* sing.

And what some voices do best is versatility. A smaller theater can say, This singer can do *Don Pasquale, L'Elisir D'Amore* and

Die Entführung aus dem Serail. Terrific! Or, This lady can sing Aida and Marguerite. Maybe she's not our perfect Aida, but we need one to do both.

Modern Repertoire

In your search for repertoire, don't neglect the contemporary operas. Sometimes a young singer with a strong personality can tap into the modern repertoire beautifully and not reveal the kind of line he or she doesn't have. It's quite amazing how voices that do not seem to fit into standard *Butterfly-Bohème-Rigoletto* repertoire find gorgeous homes in an American piece of music. If you want a nice surprise, tape yourself doing something dramatic and interesting in English, and then tape yourself doing another aria in Italian. See if you don't find what a natural performer you are in one and what an unnatural performer you may be in the other. We're becoming richer and richer in very singable contemporary music. So really research this repertoire. And you can use the experience of interacting in your own language; carry it over when working in other languages.

Frequently Asked Questions

A common question concerns whether a singer without a particularly Italianate sound, a lyric tenor perhaps, should work on something like *L'Elisir D'Amore* for auditioning purposes, where the chances are very high that the more Italian sound will get the role. My answer is to work on it, because it helps you develop what you don't have. It is, however, not the aria to start with in your audition process. We don't show off what we don't have. The first singing teacher I ever played for said, "If you don't have the *décolleté*, don't wear it." Sing an American aria first. Sing French, sing German, sing something by Benjamin Britten that really personalizes the color of your voice. Once you've done that, one of your choices can be *Elisir*. If they want it, they'll ask for it. For "getting hired" purposes, it's really good to do what you do best.

Another question concerns the advisability of singing obscure music in an audition. My experience is, if you sing such music, judges tend to listen to the music with great interest, taking the focus off you, the singer. On the other hand, obscure music can be a great help in hiding a few flaws if you're not vocally in the best of condition. The bottom line is, always sing what represents you the best. My favorite question to ask a coaching student is, "Why are you singing this?" The answer often is, "I need an aria in English (or French or Italian)." This is valid, but decide what it is you hope to achieve with the aria. It is preferable to say, "It is what I do best. It shows me off."

When a piece in English is required at an audition, be clever and inventive. One alternative is to sing something in translation, and chances are, the opera company is not asking for an English aria unless they're doing something in English. You'd be wise to know what that opera is. Do they perform operas written in English, or are they doing something in translation? In a contest or competition, if the judges want to hear how you do in English, something in translation would be fine. However, there are more and more exciting contemporary operas available today. It is a valuable experience to research these operas and learn something that was written in English.

Eventually, your voice will reach its final growth. After singing a particular repertoire for a number of years, you have a choice of whether or not to go on to a more dramatic repertoire, which can be very interesting and which lots of singers do. Singers approach bigger repertoire for many reasons: musical curiosity, desire to explore the dramatic and musical depths of that music, or let's face it — boredom. Singers are human, and after a twenty-five year career of singing *I Puritani*, often a successful tenor wants to try Otello. Whether a singer should or shouldn't continue into a bigger repertoire is a very personal question which can only be answered by the singer, along with a teacher and coaches. However, these steps shouldn't be taken until proper vocal maturity has been reached.

Repertoire is your steppingstone to the rich worlds of music and your own vocal life, but growth in repertoire is not something to be rushed. Learn what your music has to teach you before moving on.

※   ※   ※

Chapter Four

The Language

Translation. Do it. Just do it. And then redo it.

Opera is not only an intellectual form, but an emotional and very human one. A voice can express enormous humanity and an incredible range of emotions. For these reasons, a singer must understand much more than the general meaning in the text. One cannot sing in generalities. Each word has to become a real word, specific and intense, and you cannot just know what the sentence means. I repeat: *it is not enough to know what the sentence means*.

Understanding the Text

When I say to a singer, "Will you translate this for me?" the answer is invariably, "Oh, sure, just let me get my music." From that statement, I have to assume that the singer has not yet absorbed the *meaning*. Not only do you have to internalize the text so that it seems as though you have been speaking these words all your life, but the words themselves have to provoke emotional responses within you. Which means that when you translate, you cannot *only* translate word for word. "*Si*" — "yes." "*Mi chiamano*" — "they call me." "*Si*" might be, "yes," "well," "okay," "gee." "*Mi chiamano*" could be "My friends call me," "They call me," "I've always been called." Not just one word or phrase. This is especially true in the translation of adjectives: the richer, the better.

When you look in a dictionary, there are perhaps four definitions for a word. Instead of just writing down one definition, write down all four. Use all four definitions and then create an image of what that word feels like, looks like, tastes like. The same way your nose recognizes the smell of an Italian restaurant, your emotional being has to recognize the emotional quality of a word like *orrore*.

Even though you don't speak the language, and we cannot require of singers that they fluently speak four languages — they usually haven't got the time — the internalization of a word can be done all day long by just using it in place of the English one. "Ah, that's a very *bella* dress." Make these words into pictures, use them, make them your own. As a student, make the in-depth study of language a large part of your undergraduate work. This is the very best time to begin building your vocabulary and enriching your knowledge of language.

Finding the Nuances

Sometimes the large dictionaries are good for giving you the shadings of words. A dictionary that has synonyms is excellent. Or even better, a person who has a real in-depth knowledge of the language and the way it's used, such as a professor of poetry in French or Italian, can give you all the colors of the word. (And don't waste your time asking this person to only give a general sentence translation.) You can use the excellent translation books or the libretti included with recordings for general ideas.

For instance, *godiamo*, a word which appears in the "Brindisi," Act I, of *La Traviata*, has a very sensual connotation. You might ask your expert to tell you about the verb *godere*. How is that word used? Can I use it about cauliflower, or should I use it about sex? Tell me about the word *piacere*. Does it have to do with "mildly pleasing" or does it have to do with "enjoyable?" Give me ten sentences with this word.

A construction such as that used by Germont in *La Traviata* — *"Il padre in me vedete"* — is formal and ponderous, purposely so. It doesn't say, "I am Alfredo's father." It says, "In me, you see the personage of . . ." It has a special significance, connotation and weight.

Then there is the "Voi che sapete" of Cherubino — "You who know." If you look up "to know" in the Shakespearean dictionary, the meaning includes, "to have carnal knowledge of," not only "to be acquainted." *Sapere* means "to know" and *conoscere* means "to know." So why didn't Mozart use *conoscere*? And notice how Mozart always goes up in the music on the word "know." *Amor* could be many things — love, desire, sex. The word *cor* as used by Cherubino means "heart," but the heart can be in a lot of places. *Provare* in Italian means "to rehearse"; it also means "to feel." So it's not just a word, but a combination of word and idea. *"Quello ch'io provo vi ridorò e per me nuovo capir nol so,"* Cherubino says. "That which I want to do over again I think about and rehearse in my mind." What is he thinking about? What does he want to rehearse?

In *Così Fan Tutte*, there are obvious double entendres when the women talk about how big the men's noses and feet are. Yes, opera is often about sex. As a great acting teacher, Ludwig Donath, said, *"Don Giovanni* is about sex, sex, sex and a little murder." The same can be said for many operas: they are non-vulgarly, healthfully, youthfully about sex. And if we're not used to working with the text enough to enjoy this beautiful, refreshing approach, we miss it. Cherubino is a great example of this: he doesn't say *"di ne notte,"* he says *"notte ne di"* — "I can't find any peace of mind night nor day." Somehow, night always comes first to Cherubino. And when you look at Zerlina's aria, "Batti, batti," in *Don Giovanni*, she also says *"notte e di."* Mozart obviously enjoyed "night and day" more than "day and night!"

The Mechanics of Translation and Subtext

What I find helpful is to gather an excellent dictionary and paper and pencil. Write out your text and, as you do, say it out loud. By the time you've written a double consonant, i.e., the two b's in *babbo*, you've also said them in just the right way. Or the two n's in *vanno*. And your mouth begins to get used to saying these words as a string of consonants and vowels, as your eyes see them and your hand writes them.

Skip several lines on your page so you can write three or four meanings for each word, the richest meanings you can. Underneath that, write an English sentence. And underneath that, write a very colloquial sentence that reflects your own personality or the subtext. Use modern, everyday words — words *you* might use. When you do this, the whole process has much less chance of being vague, it becomes more precise and gives your own flavor to the meaning of the words. This gives you additional resources.

Let's take apart some of the language of "Musetta's Waltz" from *La Bohème* for meaning and subtext.

"Quando m'en vo . . ."

"When I take myself out . . ."

(He knows when you take yourself out, Musetta, you always put on your sexiest dress.)

"Soletta . . ."

"All alone . . ."

(Without you, darling.)

"Per la via . . ."

"On the boulevard . . ."

(Not on the back streets where you take me.)

"La gente sosta e' mira."

"The people just stop and look."

(They just stop and look at my dress, the one you didn't buy me.)

You can be more inventive than the obvious meanings. And ask yourself, What did Puccini mean when he wrote about a woman's "hidden" beauty? Followed by *"e tu che sai"* — "you who know where that hidden beauty is." Notice a form of the verb *sapere* again.

"Che memorie ti struggi . . ." One of the meanings of *struggere* is when the seventeenth person in line cuts in front of you, and you can't do anything about it.

At the end of Musetta's Waltz, *". . . ma ti senti morir"* is a phrase for being very aroused and involved sexually or sexually frustrated. It has nothing to do with really dying. It is tastefully sensual.

You need to translate your languages into your being and into your heart, your eyes. You begin on paper; you end in your imagination.

Plugging a foreign word into an emotion is something few other people in theatrical world have to do. This makes learning acting as an opera singer different from other forms of theater, and quite a bit more complicated. There's not only a strange language, but also the singing to deal with! Even if you study acting with a fine teacher, you still have to deal with traveling through another language in order to get at an emotional system. And *emotion* is what carries meaning. So ask yourself if you are singing in the language, not translating as you sing. Speak your piece through in English a few times, then in the original language a few times. Set up a chain of thoughts between the words in the aria or song and your thoughts in natural English.

I highly recommend the William Weaver libretti and *The Ring of Words* by Philip L. Miller to give you a whole idea of what's going on in a piece. What's nice about the Weaver books is that on the page opposite the libretto, he writes the translation out in full, not hyphenated as in the music. This is important, because the words become easily readable and more real. Read them into your tape recorder, really making an actor's sense out of them, and hear yourself saying those words as words, sentences and phrases. Then you'll find that the phrasing in your singing becomes much more automatic.

Translating the Entire Opera

So much for the audition arias. But what do you do in a full opera when your colleague is singing, and you don't understand a blessed word of what he's saying? And what's more, you simply can't memorize all of his or her words, because you have to do this opera in a month, and it would take you seven years to digest all that translation!

Well, get the libretto, and find a word you understand. "*Intendo,*" let's say. It means "to understand," "to comprehend." So now you can listen to a sentence and react to the word "*intendo.*" You can learn two words out of every sentence or out of every two sentences that your colleague sings and react to those words. "*Finalmente mia,*" Scarpia says. Tosca, you know what that means. Circle the easy words, the strong words, the words that appeal to you emotionally. Learn those, and associate a reaction. Later on, the stage director may agree or disagree, but the word will have some significant meaning. With each rehearsal and performance that you do, you will add more words, and by the time you're on your tenth repetition, you're well on your way to understanding everything that your colleague says. That way, you're really becoming an integrated part of the performance.

Without this type of work, as we have seen in so many performances and videotapes, it becomes obvious who is on the stage just waiting to react, instead of truly understanding while the other person is singing. On a videotape, you see that the camera generally moves away from those people. The audience in the theater does not have that choice. Go to a performance of a Broadway show, and see what it looks like when everybody understands what's being said. Go to an original-language performance of, say, *Il Barbiere di Siviglia*, when half the cast is Italian and half is American, and you often have no trouble seeing who understands and who does not.

Pronunciation and Diction

The second component of language is, of course, the pronunciation/diction component. There are those singers who are extraordinarily gifted linguistically, and then there are those who really have to work. But excellent pronunciation and diction can be achieved by almost everyone. It gets back to the idea of controlling what you can versus worrying about what you cannot. Be great at what's possible. Okay, tenor, maybe you can't be 6'2", but you can communicate with great success. Maybe you don't have a good high C yet. But there are other things you can have, such as imaginative, musical, stylistic phrasing and the ability to produce music that is very expressive. These elements are really based on understanding the language.

I was once involved in auditions for *Madama Butterfly* with an Italian conductor. We listened to ten different people, and not one of them could sing Italian acceptably for the maestro. Put yourself in his shoes. Supposing you went to see a production of

Oklahoma! and heard Curly sing, "Oh Vat a Bootiful Mornink?" Many, if not most young American singers sound like Americans singing in French or Italian or German. Every school gives a few months of pronunciation classes, during which time you can just about learn that there is such a thing. There are also lots and lots of books (better than nothing). But books can't hear you.

At the most basic level, you need to know where to double the consonant in Italian and where you can't, when you have to shorten a vowel in German, when you have to slightly change a vowel in French to make it rhyme with a vowel that preceded it, how open the "schwa" vowel has to be. All of these things are extraordinarily important! It's also very interesting to take an aria, maybe one from *La Bohème*, as sung by three different tenors, tape the renditions and listen to each one of them. Listen to the Italian singer, the American — whomever you find — and notice what they do. Then read some very good books on diction. Colorni has written an extremely helpful one. The *Zingarelli* dictionary is absolutely indispensable; it has all the words written out in the International Phonetic Alphabet (IPA) and gives you all the open and closed sounds. An open or closed vowel can completely change the meaning of a word. Take a look at the list of words that cause phrasal doubling, that is, the internal doubling of the initial consonant. Then go back to your recordings and make yourself aware of phrasal doublings; for example, "E *t*ardi" (*La Traviata*), me *p*overetta (*La Bohème*). If you can't afford this wonderful dictionary, ask for it for Christmas or your birthday.

English is a language in which we bounce off our consonants when we are angry: "I could *k*ill him." Italians, to express that kind of emotion, go for the vowel: "I k*ee*l you." Intense emotion in the Italian language is carried by the vowels. "*Quando m'en vo.*" Make those vowels long! Then you can go easily into the consonant, making it resonant, and then go right away into the next vowel. In order to bring emphasis to a word in Italian, you can just change the pitch. Each one of these different arrangements of pitches holds a great deal of meaning and replaces the need to make heavy accents. This type of intensive work will do wonders for your legato. The presence of vowel thrown next to vowel with a clear, sharp consonant in between is what makes this type of singing so gorgeous.

Tom Grubb's book, *Singing in French*, is another effective tool. Immerse yourself slowly in this book, and he will help you learn the difference between French and Italian music and language. Jeannine Reiss is a marvelous French diction coach. When you see her name on the back of a recording, you're going to be listening to good French. So many young singers are tempted to close off their voices when singing in French. I admit it's perhaps not the easiest language in the world to sing at first, but by exposing yourself to the wonderful teaching of Grubb, the coaching of Reiss, and the singing of artists such as Regine Crespin, you have an excellent start on recognizing what good, well-sung French sounds like.

A Good Example

Talking about vowels and reading about them on the page are not nearly the same as hearing them or doing them. Each language has its proper vocalic placement in the same way that French, Italian and German restaurants have their particular aroma. Vowel sounds are something that can only truly be taught by somebody sitting with you.

Listen to a recording of someone whose pronunciation is impeccable. Sherrill Milnes' Italian is wonderful. Nicolai Gedda's pronunciation is flawless. Callas's Italian is expressive and beautiful. Gwyneth Jones' German is masterful. Record them. Record you. Tape Freni singing "Mi chiamano Mimi." When you hear *"A tela o a seta ricamo in casa e fuori"* — a line that most young sopranos usually turn backward and inside out — see if your vowels sound like the vowels you're hearing on the recording. If you approach each language as if you were about to make your debut at La Scala, you'll make very strict rules for yourself.

It's easy to say, "Well, you know, So and So's (famous star) Italian was never really . . ." To all statements like this, I have only one thing to say: if your voice is just as extraordinary — okay. But make sure you are vocally in that category before you say, "I don't really have to work on my acting, phrasing, music, language, diction or pronunciation."

If you don't have access to somebody who can really go through the language in a precise way, what are your options? One is to pretend you're five years old and read syllable by syllable, as slowly and as beautifully as you can. With the use of a cassette tape, you can make use of pronunciation by mail from an expert who lives far away from you. Learn the names of the top language coaches, look for their names on recordings and utilize their language expertise.

There is a lot of help available, many master classes, many situations in which you can learn the rules of language. If you are serious about this business of singing, you can expect language to be one of the biggest components.

The frequent use of subtitles in performances these days does afford you more opportunity to work in an original language, which is, of course, better for the voice. Despite this advantage, you still must work on the absorption of text and on the vocal, emotional and physical ability to deliver it. This absorption comes together with style, knowledge and skill.

Language is not something you just pick up and do. Each language has a style. Italian, with its lack of "schwa" vowels; French, with its varied hues and colors of vowels; German, with its "schwa" vowels and umlauts — all need to be carefully looked into. Never mind that we're also singing opera in

Czechloslovakian and Russian!

Don't Forget English

And what about the command of your own language? Just because it's your language doesn't mean you don't have to study it. In English, singers fight to emphasize consonants more and more. Consonants are important, but one of the biggest problems is understanding the vowels. It's a fallacy that English isn't clear only because of consonants. Also, many singers do not put enough emphasis on the "hummed" and "sung-through" sounds: "ths," "n," "m," and "l." More attention to IPA is helpful. English works like any other language, except it's not spelled out. In the decision of which IPA symbol to use, you achieve more of an understanding of what the vowel is *supposed* to be. Take apart the diphthongs. For "I know" — write "Ai-ee no-u." In IPA: "Ai nou." Go through a piece several times slowly. This is the way non-English-speaking singers learn English. For reference, both Madeleine Marshall and Dorothy Uris have written good books on English diction.

There is no reason to burden yourself with poor pronunciation and poor diction. When you're too young to work yourself intensively vocally, work yourself intensively linguistically. Go right ahead and do it.

※　　※　　※

Chapter Five

The Music

Simple things. Melody, rhythm, harmony. Simple. But so easily overlooked, ill-prepared and under-enjoyed.

When studying music, it is best to do it right the first time. Otherwise, there is nothing that comes back as quickly as your first mistake. So let's avoid the first mistake. Get a good foundation in your arias *now*. Otherwise, fixing them can be a most tiresome, expensive and frustrating proceeding. If you don't learn it right the first time, you can pay your coach year after year to correct you. Sometimes I find myself making circles around the circles I made last year.

The key to learning a piece of music correctly and wisely, in my opinion, is in knowing *how* to study. Many singers set aside an hour or two a day and sing through their pieces. They stop and start, but still, they are working on each *entire* piece, rather than finding a style of study that really works. There are many ways. Ask advice, look around, try different things.

For instance, try this. Sing through the aria once for fun. Then, start really *working* on it. Dissect it. Work on small sections of four bars at a time, eight bars a day, examining in depth every detail of those measures. Then put them together. It's so much more cost-efficient in terms of labor and helps you not to miss any important features of the piece.

When beginning your study of a piece of music, never, but never, sing anything without going to the library, finding the orchestra score and reading the fifteen or so pages on which your aria is written. It doesn't take long. Compare the dots on your notes to the dots on the notes in the score. Compare the words, compare the phrasing, compare the bowing, so that you can see when the violins play with you and when the French horn does. That *p* can stand for many different things. Know what they are! There's nothing like seeing the music spread out in the orchestra score and noticing all the different instruments the piano represents. Then the accompaniment becomes understandable. And, of course, you will check pitch for pitch, note for note, against the music you're using.

Errors in the Music

There are some horrendous mistakes, musical and verbal, in some of the musical anthologies. One of my personal favorites is the bass, in "Infelice! E tuo credevi" in Act I of *Ernani*, who speaks of the eyebrow on a portion of his anatomy with the immortal line, "*Si bel ciglio immaculato,*" instead of "*giglio immacolato.*" Had you translated the aria, you would most certainly know "*ciglio immaculato*" could not *possibly* be correct!

Then there was the soprano who sang "Pace, pace mio dio" from *La Forza del Destino*, and I said to her, "Have you ever heard this before?" "Yes, many times." "Did you ever notice that other sopranos are singing different notes from the ones you're singing at the end?" "No." There were wrong notes printed in her book.

We have new versions, old versions and revised versions of

many scores today. There are new versions of operas coming out all the time. Many Rossini and Verdi scores are being revised. How nice it would be if you could take advantage of all this right from the beginning of your studies. Take the time to compare everything that's written in your score. In the "Ballatella" from *I Pagliacci*, for instance, the accompaniment is incomplete as it is written in the piano version. Write it out for your pianists. Baritones singing "Avant des quitter ces lieu," Valentine's aria in *Faust* — there's a whole other world to be added in the accompaniment of the aria. Write it in your book so the pianist will play it. Almost all the scores have a major mistake in the accompaniment of the Micaela-Don José duet. In "Depuis le jour" from *Louise*, there are very important tempi markings missing that you can find in the score. There are also accompaniment figures missing that make the aria easier to sing. It is critical that you have a good coach who can advise you in these matters.

Practice Time

You will evolve your own work style, but as I mentioned, I highly recommend a slow study of a few measures at a time. I think it's far better to take four bars of music and look at them for five to ten minutes on the clock, really studying their internal structure, harmony, melody, their reason for being, the commas — every single fly speck in those four bars — until the questions begin to come to your mind. Why is this rhythm like this? Why is this bar like that? What do they mean? Four bars today, four bars tomorrow, four bars the next day. You can study your trills for five minutes, then walk around the piano. Another five minutes, a cup of tea, in no way exhausting yourself. But in a week, with four bars of really thoughtful work a day, you will have that piece so well thought out that you can really begin to sing it. You will practically have it memorized. You have no chance of putting an "r" in a wrong place. In half an hour, you can study sixteen bars, which is a great deal. Singers always seem to feel the need to spend fifteen minutes singing a piece from beginning to end. I don't think that helps when you are beginning to study.

Continuous work is important, even if you put in just half an hour each day. Most of you have jobs or go to school all day, and of course, you're tired. But try physical exercise in the morning, then a vocal warm-up and technique exercises, and soon you will be asking, Is it this vowel or that vowel that needs work? on the way to the stockroom. At lunch time, run into a church and do a little work on your vocal technique. Come home, have a little dinner and do a little exercise, and either take out the tape your pianist made for you or go to your pianist, even for half an hour. If you feel fine, sing your pieces. If you don't feel that energetic, mark a few of the high notes and work out the problems of the other pieces. Is this legato enough? Does this require a portamento? Did I do too much? Did I begin my first note properly? Did I end my last note properly? If you're too tired to sing, there's always language or translation.

People are busier now than ever before. But you can make the time to do anything you want, *if* you learn how to use your time effectively. Buses, subways, planes, taxis and streetcars are good places to read the history you need in order to do an opera, to work on translation, to listen to language tapes, to listen to music tapes, aria in hand. Time sitting on the couch is great for watching and analyzing performance videos. Use the available half-hour here and there, or even the available fifteen minutes, to vocalize, to work on a translation, to study coloratura, trills, etc. And within all of this, yes, there has to be time completely *away* from study and from the opera business. It is essential to recharge. And you'll be surprised, after a day or a weekend or an evening free of study and concentration, how fresh your approach is when you return to the work.

Rhythm and Tempo

So many young singers lose track of some of the most central issues. First of all, the how of everything and secondly, the why of everything. It saddens me to find somebody who has never discovered the joy of what we teach all five-year-olds to do when we teach them to play the piano — count. But somehow, as soon as many musicians start to sing, counting becomes secondary. When you remove the spine of the musical skeleton, the same thing will happen to the music that will happen if you remove the spine from your body: you will be left in a rather unflattering heap.

Finding the tempo is another important element. You have to see the tempo, the speed of the music, as a bicycle that you can peddle faster or slower as you want. Go smoothly into the changes. Verdi's sixteenth notes, dotted eighth notes or triplets are little maps of the emotions which provoked those rhythms. The tempo at which these rhythms move changes their emotional messages to the audience.

Tempo is also important for the movement of your own individual voice. Does your voice need a slower tempo, a faster tempo, does this phrase need to move ahead? How will you plan out the tempo in order to breathe easier here, and not have to breathe there?

The music must have an inner rhythmic structure. We can be extraordinarily sophisticated about rhythms, or we can be extremely simple. But the pattern is like the biological rhythms in our bodies. Our heartbeat is so necessary, speeding up and slowing down, that we don't even think about it. And the same with the rhythms of music. The people who have not taken the time to count and study the rhythm of the recitative to "Sempre libera" from *La Traviata* have missed an enormously perceptive composer's feeling of emotions translated into rhythm.

Understanding the immense importance of the rhythms, tempi and the relationship that holds the orchestra together with you and eight other people on the stage is crucial. There is no room for nearly, maybe or sort of.

Some opera houses, especially large, international ones, have a prompter. Working with a prompter is fun, because it reassures the singer that a word or a rest won't be forgotten as the performer becomes more involved in the drama, has a memory slip or any one of the thousand unexpected situations that routinely occur. However, as a beginning singer, you're not likely to have a prompter. Nor should anyone depend on the prompter in order to sing the music correctly. In addition, when you get into a bigger theater, your conductor expects you to be "on top" of the rhythm. Your sense of rhythm has to be secure enough to sing *ahead*, so that you are with the orchestra. The stage is large, and the orchestra pit is often big as well. Sound takes time to travel, and the further back on the stage you go, the more you must anticipate. The conductor has a lot of responsibility and many facets of a performance that need his attention. If you can't stay with him, you may find yourself being dismissed or simply not rehired. A coach who has had a great deal of experience in a theater and working with conductors can advise and assist you in preparing to work with a conductor and orchestra. It will be unusual to find a conductor who doesn't allow you to discuss tempi, particularly where your vocal necessities are involved, but you both owe each other the most meticulous rhythmical preparation.

Even the youngest singer has the ability to dissect rhythm. Count, conduct your pieces, figure out what kind of motions this conductor is going to go through. Go to a performance and watch the conductor. Sing along with the singers (in your head, of course!). Find a recording. Conduct it. Locate a student conductor or young professional, and ask him or her to conduct you through an aria. See what kinds of problems you encounter. Begin to establish for yourself the ways in which beats, as units of time, look and feel and, most importantly, what they mean. The aria from *Werther* is a wonderful example: "Je devrais les detruire." The last two syllables of *"detruire"* are a dotted rhythm. In my opinion, these have to be sung as written to show Charlotte's uncertainty. She's saying, "Do I have to destroy these?" This is a spot that lends itself to carelessness and, when done incorrectly, can change the intention to one of absolute certainty: "I have to destroy these." The correct rhythm makes it so clear that the audience understands.

I'm also not talking about a solfége prison. I'm talking about the spine of the music, the process that allows it to be flexible, that allows it to move, to go forward, that allows your breath to find its way of supporting you in the arch of the melody and enables you to build the frame over which to put your canvas. The architecture of the music has to be so completely *understood* that what the composer intended is accurately transmitted.

Look at how much information you can perceive just from the attitude of somebody's spine. You can get as much information from whether the rhythm is sixteeth notes or half notes. And here, the singer has full emotional choice. Why is this rhythm this way? It's up to you. So count. Write the numbers in your book. Don't be ashamed. Buy a new piece of music if you don't want your teachers to see it. Your music is your work paper, your workbook. You will discover the rich imagination that you have as you ponder the rhythms and absorb how they are and why they are. When we discuss reasons for the emotional whys of the rhythms, there are very few ways to be wrong.

It was for a while a tradition, especially among Italian voice teachers and conductors that I was so fortunate to work with, to say, No, my dear, it goes like this. And you did it like this, and that was that, no questions. It was valuable to get the benefit of their experience and brilliant insights into the music, but there is a difference between learning the music with integrity and just being "correct." After all, being merely correct is not the point; we don't become artists to play it safe. We bemoan the lack of grand personality in singers today; this is part of the high price to be paid for being so "correct." When we allow singers to study only in this fashion, we end up with the vanilla soprano, the homogenized mezzo, the blank baritone and the behaviorless bass. Unless we protect that combination of the singer's personality and the personality of the music, which always and eternally strike different sparks together, we rob ourselves of new interpretations and a great deal of new insight into the music.

Putting your personality, your imagination, your emotions into your music, together with the insights and experience of others, is essential. But don't etch your decisions in stone. Establish flexible opinions, because for all of your life, you'll find a conductor who does it another way and a director who does it a third way. And each time, the combination will produce new and exciting results.

Harmony

Really get acquainted with harmony. Let somebody play the music through for you or play it yourself. Remember all those hours spent in Harmony class? Now is the time to reap the benefit of all the work you put into those classes. Hear and rehear the pieces that are all too familiar and find what's new and wonderful in the harmonies. Learn how the harmonies speak to you emotionally.

For instance, for sopranos who sing Pamina's aria, "Ach, ich fühls" from *Die Zauberflöte*, renew your acquaintanceship with the *incredible* dissonance in the harmony and chromatics of the harmonic structure; the chords that don't go where you expect them, except that you've heard this aria so often, you thoroughly expect them to go there. In *La Bohème*, at the end of the aria "Addio, senza rancor," that little modulation after *"Se vuoi, se vuoi ..."* is such a surprise! If you had never heard it before, you would have goose bumps all over. Let the pianist play it so it sounds new again. Re-listen, re-think, re-find. It requires that you be very quiet and open your ears to what's there.

Cherubino's aria again affords a wonderful example of seeing and hearing what's really in the music. It's a familiar aria, yet when you realize the subject matter about which the pubescent Cherubino is singing and then look at the music, you have a wealth of understanding of this aria and of the reasons for the harmonic structure and can bring so much more to it as a performer. "This is all new for me . . ." goes into a minor chord and ends in a major chord on "understand." Look at the music underneath, at what Mozart did with major and minor chords and putting notes together.

One fun mental exercise I like to do with my students is what I call the "five-year-old." I learned this from a fine soprano and a lot of five-year-olds. Children go straight to the emotional heart of the music. Do a five-year-old exercise for yourself. Listen to individual chords in the music. If you were five, what would the chords, harmonic sequences and rhythm make you do? What is your instinctive response? Is it a peeking-out-from-behind-the-door chord, a scary chord, a surprising one? Does it make you slow down, speed up, mope in a chair? Which animal would you be to this music? Take the response to its adult conclusion. Out of this comes the kernel of what you will refine and use. Your instinct is great — use it!

This is an excellent exercise for finding transitions and for discovering the exaggerations, as in Dorabella's aria from *Così Fan*

Tutte. It gives you what's intrinsic in the *music*. As another example, if you played part of Cherubino's aria for a five-year-old, the child would dance, skip, jump, giggle, laugh. What would a five-year-old do with the "Maledizione" theme of *Rigoletto*? Be frightened. You can find your way so easily and so honestly into the character of the music by using your musically sensitive, unencumbered, emotionally responsive five-year-old self.

Melody

Melody is the easiest thing to learn by ear, unfortunately. You say, Yes, sure, I know how Mimi's aria goes or how "La donna é mobile" goes. Do I know that's an augmented fourth? What augmented fourth? Do I know what note it is? Is it an E, F, G? Why? Does it make any difference? Yes! Whether it's a B or B flat makes a *big* difference to a singer.

I once played *I Vespri Siciliani* for a famous singer who stopped, looked at the keyboard and asked me why I was playing a high C sharp under the cadenza. I said, "Because it is C sharp." She said, "It can't be. I can't sing that note." Well, she'd been singing it for the past ten minutes or more. So maybe sometimes it's better not to know. But knowing what pitch you're on and what key you're in, 99 percent of the time, is a very good idea. It's not a detriment to good singing. And knowing what it looks like instead of what it sounds like can be very helpful. Look at it first, before your voice gets in there. Your voice is expensive. Save it. Listen to the aria a few times. Let your brain and your vocal technique and your ear absorb what these pitches are before you sing them. Don't just do something over again. Think first. Think very carefully. Replay it, just like the athletes do. And whatever you do, bring your belongings with you when you go to a new piece. Take what you've learned previously. You'll find it helps.

The exact opposite, however, is true for *relearning* a piece. In that case, if you put an aria away for long enough, some of the mistakes will be forgotten. Listen to new versions of it, new singers and new interpretations. Then it's a little easier to relearn.

Dynamics and Embellishments

Each piece of music has its own momentum. You can't stop to check and criticize yourself, or the momentum will be lost. Sing with conviction. Sing it as if you're right, whether you are or not. There must be a reason for each fermata, each crescendo, each diminuendo. Make your choices and commit yourself to them. Rests in music aren't for resting. You can use rests to such an advantage. They can be where atmosphere is created or only the invisible seams that connect emotion to emotion. Give emotional meaning to dynamic markings. *Forte* can mean big, strong, juicy, voluptuous, exciting, explosive, glorious. *Piano* can mean calm, careful, whispering, or — in mid-range — not pushing or taking away sound. It doesn't, on the other hand, indicate undersinging or using a weak or threadbare tone.

"Appoggiatura" comes from the verb *appoggiare*, to lean. Mozart, Rossini and Donizetti are among the many composers that stylistically require the use of appoggiaturas. They are used to make the recitative line more melodic and will, therefore, show many different emotional facets: weakness, vulnerability, strength or charm.

Appoggiaturas are highly personal in their use. At first, it's best to learn your recitatives without many appoggiaturas, and then later, add the ones you think are appropriate, always being ready to change for the conductor. The one thing that is for sure is that each conductor with whom you work will want something different with regard to appoggiaturas. Ultimately, the text is the best guide.

Appoggiaturas are a wonderful subject for an entire book.

There are many, many great singers and conductors of tradition that you can listen to and whose example you can follow. However, appoggiaturas are a source of much debate and discussion, and in this book, I can only make you aware of them. I suggest that you read some of the new books and articles that have resulted from the excellent research being done on the classical and bel canto periods of music.

"Portamento" is an important stylistic device in Italian music, often abused, but very important to be done correctly, with good support and with good energy. Listen carefully to singers who use their portamenti very well and don't merely slide from one note to another or scoop. (Sliding, scooping and portamento are not all the same thing.) A portamento requires the same energy with which you *lift* a priceless Ming vase. You can use a portamento when it helps the voice technically, or when two notes are connected with the same vowel, or when marked, or when tradition says you use them. Most conductors prefer that we almost never use portamenti in Mozart. Portamento in bel canto is usually late, fast and light. There are several interesting articles by Will Crutchfield on musical practices, especially on portamenti. William Ashbrook's book on Donizetti is also an excellent study tool.

Puccini requires the right kind of portamento and is almost always indicated in the music. French music requires very few. The French are much more indicative than the Italians in their manuscripts. When the French want a rest, they put in a rest, and when they want a portamento, they write in: *avec portamento*. Notice all the clear directions that Massenet wrote his music; follow them. Donizetti wrote his music with very few directions. However, these can be learned from the singers from whom we have inherited a clear indication of style; they are recorded.

A composer's individual way of writing is particularly fascinating. When you've studied a great deal of a particular composer's work, you begin to understand the way he writes and the way he uses or doesn't use written indications. You come to see where your freedom is and where you are constrained to follow the music as it's written. Puccini and Massenet write many directions, Verdi some, but we interpret from his tempi and rhythmical markings what his intentions were. Read the stage directions that are in the scores as well. They are a part of the emotional ambiance and the composer's idea of the character. This, in turn, can give us a wealth of information in terms of how strict, how tense, how loose, how free the rhythms and dynamic levels should be.

Performance Practices

Performance practice is a very interesting way of learning how fashions, ideas and tastes in music change. Find a recording from the 1940s, and listen to the musical values, the language values, the portamenti and the rests used and not used. Follow that same opera through recordings up to the 1990s. See how our idea of musical interpretation has changed. You'll see that there have been periods of time when opera was more purist, when there was less use of the traditions and closer adherence to the composer's writing, when there was more emphasis on interpretation, on voice, on musical correctness or on the drama.

It's wise to have an idea of what the performance practices are in your time, rather than discussing the right and wrong of what has been, what this conductor does or what that singer has done. It's important to know what we are trying to structure in music and what we hope to achieve with that structure. So as you will hear, portamenti in bel canto and in Mozart, as examples, will change frequently between the '50s, the '60s and the '70s. Take all the best information from all the great singers and conductors, and use it to your best advantage, always considering the time frame which you are in presently.

Phrasing

Phrasing in music is a very delicate process, something we tend not to think about in the first years of making beautiful sounds. But it's important to take an active interest in the phrasing of music. Listen to instrumentalists and how they phrase as well. The work done by violinists and wind instrumentalists can be inspiring and instructive in understanding classical and romantic phrasing. The continuity and shape of another singer's phrasing can also be an enlightening source of study. Language, music and style have so much to do with the kind of elegant phrasing that we are continuously searching for. As you listen to music, be aware of not only the composer's style of phrasing, but of each singer's. Fortunately, there is a wealth of wonderful singing to be heard: Placido Domingo's gorgeous phrasing of Italian music; Renata Scotto, with her brilliant combination of musical and textual phrasing with dramatic intensity; Montserrat Caballe and her exquisite bel canto phrasing; Carol Vaness's expert phrasing of Mozart.

Flexibility is crucial within phrasing, because singing is a very flexible process. Some days your body needs more breath than others. When singers go to Mexico or out West, they find themselves breathing more often, because there is less oxygen. When they go to Barcelona, they have so much breath they're drowning. So that's important to keep in mind. Don't impose intellectual judgements on your non-intellectual body. We don't do music exactly the same every day. Leave room to adjust musically.

A baritone friend of mine recently sang for Pavarotti, who, after listening, asked him to phrase something differently. After years of classes, this young baritone didn't stop to think, Why, what does he mean? He just did exactly what Luciano wanted. Later he understood why. If a singer can, in an audition with a conductor or another singer, demonstrate this kind of flexibility, it's wonderful. This baritone was then able to ask, Was my phrasing too choppy? This question enabled Luciano to speak with him in more detail about phrasing. That process is not only good for auditions, but is also useful when working with a conductor or manager.

Coloratura and Cadenzas

Most people can learn to sing coloratura passages. It just takes time and patience. The first thing to determine is, How good is your coloratura? Sometimes, you can just do it; some people have a faster voice than others. It doesn't always have to do with size; it sometimes has to do with mismanaged weight. A voice is never really weightless. You don't weigh less when you walk lightly, but you do balance differently.

For the hard vocalises, such as the one in "Sempre libera" in *La Traviata*, the singers I have heard do these best go through them applying all the technique they have learned — what you have to open, close, support, lift, balance, according to your technical range and skill at the moment.

Rhythm is a very big aid in learning to process cadenzas and difficult coloratura. The two problems seem to be where and how to find the articulation, and where and how to find the rhythm. The way I hear people working, and find makes some sense, is first to find the accents, the rhythm, with a metronome if necessary. Put a vamp bass underneath if it helps you. Sometimes, it's helpful just to walk around while you're practicing. It keeps your body from being too stiff. Walk, do your scales.

There are many good exercise books that encompass chromatic scales, jumps, long scales, different keys, different vowels, different patterns. You can also take your cadenzas and make vocalises out of them. Before you start out on a piece of music that has coloratura, excerpt the coloratura and study it technically first.

After grasping the rhythmical patterns, the next step is to get the pitches very clean in your mind. Sometimes I hear singers using to very good advantage an articulation device, such as an "n" or "m," something that will separate one note from another. The articulation device can be one for each note — na-na-na-na — then two together — na-a, na-a — then three together, etc. Varying ways of putting those notes back and forth seem to really loosen up the mind and body: short-long-long, short-long-short-long, and so on.

Another device that will sometimes help your voice bounce a little is to do the coloratura in a staccato manner. Listen to any Queen of the Night and you'll understand in a second how exposed pitches are when staccato. Your ear has to carry you into the pitch, so you have to know *exactly* what it is. In the staccato, don't go too fast at first. Line up the pitches very clearly and hear them carefully, because the intervals are sometimes awkward. It can be four whole steps and one half, two half-steps and one whole. That kind of coloratura singing is like being a sharpshooter — it's either 100 percent right or 100 percent wrong. You have to know where to aim.

I find that short, frequent periods of practice — five to fifteen minutes every hour, particularly for this type of work — are sensational. Gradually, increase the rhythms, and if they're not steady, use the metronome. Pieces that are really difficult to sing, like the Queen of the Night, can really benefit from mental imaging and hearing yourself sing it, and then actually doing it. Think, then do, rather than do, do, do. And work with your teachers on getting the breath and body buoyant, so you don't feel locked up or locked in.

It's helpful to know where your voice moves the fastest. That enables you choose the kind of music with which you want to show off and the kind you want to grow into. Some voices will work faster in the middle, some in the top. If you're going to sing Semiramide, it's important to know if you have middle coloratura. Then there's the high coloratura, like Queen of the Night, or the big lyric roles of Mozart, which have fairly high tessituras. You need to be sure you can sustain that with ease and fluency.

Recitatives

Recitatives are the subject of entire classes, so obviously all that is involved in them can't be encompassed in part of a chapter! Recitatives have to be treated stylistically. Silly as it sounds, it's imperative to look at whose name is in the upper right corner before you study a recitative. Mozart recitatives, Bellini recitatives, Donizetti recitatives, Verdi recitatives — all are in many ways extraordinarily different. One way to help yourself is to listen to recordings of great conductors and great singers, and familiarize yourself with the *sound* of different kinds of recitatives. It's also very good to study the recitatives of modern composers such as Britten and Menotti, in order to study recitatives in one's own language. This can help you deal with recitatives in other languages.

The second thing is to recognize that recitatives come from the word *recitare*, "to recite." The major emphasis shifts to what's being *said* rather than sung. Any attempt to do a recitative without the most intimate knowledge of the words will be disastrous.

The next big division comes between the *secco* recitatives (with harpsichord, or harpsichord and cello, that is, without much underneath the singer) and the *accompaniato* recitatives. The fewer instruments accompanying the recitative, the more freely the recitative can be treated. The *secco* recitatives are the ones most closely related to what's happening on the stage — they are Mozart and Rossini recitatives, by and large. These *secco* recitatives are inevitably in 4/4 time. We should understand that human beings do not speak in 4/4 time; however, the written rhythms are as close to speech as the composer could get them.

Find a group of singers interested in doing recitatives. Examine the opera in terms of who speaks faster and who speaks slower. This will differ with each person's opinion of the character. If we're discussing *Il Barbiere di Siviglia*, perhaps we see Figaro as the fastest-speaking and Bartolo as the slowest. There's room for lots of opinions. Once you establish a basic speech speed, vary that. Use lots of rubato. Go faster and slower to change the speech pattern inside a particularly long section. Be sure that your cues are always picked up quickly from the person singing before you, unless you purposely want to make a "stage wait." Otherwise, we need to move the recitatives along. By that, I don't mean go quickly. I mean, use varying speeds, by all means, but don't leave big spaces before and after your line.

Read recitatives in the original language, and then in your own language. Work them as a dialogue, using your natural instincts to help you move physically. I can't stress enough the importance of interaction in recitatives. Learning to communicate and react to the other person's lines is a critical part of learning the style of recitative. More and more, when you're being considered for an opera with a lot of recitative, recitative is included in your audition. Singers often hear, "Yes, start the aria from the recitative, please." Your ability to handle this form fluently is essential.

And Finally . . .

Some of the things that it's not possible to deal with in a book are, for instance, What is the right style for Gilda? Are these cadenzas right for you, or should you sing it the way it's written? Should you sing the E flat at the end of "Sempre libera" or as written? There are lots of choices. What is the perfect tempo for "De' miei bollenti spiriti" from *La Traviata*? To answer these questions, especially if you are a young and relatively inexperienced singer, you have to find a knowledgeable coach in order to learn what the rules are and, at the same time, keep your individuality. When you're out there on the stage without us, your instinct, brain and training are what must bring you through. But to know the length of time to hold a note, or how dark or bright that note should be, requires the helpf of ears other than your own.

Our ideas are precious to us, but if they don't work, we must change them. Don't be afraid to throw away last year's ideas. If you don't know what to do, use your imagination and do the best you can. It will be better than nothing. But don't accept stereotyped, routine, predictable ideas, especially from yourself. Know how to go about digesting musical information so that it becomes part of you. And don't forget that ideas come from the simple things: melody, rhythm, harmony.

᳇   ᳇   ᳇

Chapter Six

Analyze, Don't Criticize

One of the very best things I've ever found for a singer to do is to ask him or herself, "What do I really like about my voice, and what do I know about my voice?" It's a question I've asked nine thousand times in my classes, and I have probably twice in my life had a singer come back with an answer like, "My voice has a bright quality," "My voice is beautiful," "My voice has a wide range," or "What's good about my voice is its flexibility." Most singers say, "My acting is . . ." "No," I interrupt, "your voice." "Well, my energy . . ." "*No.* Your voice."

All young singers want their voices to be thought of as beautiful. They will tell us they want to be thought of as a brilliant actor, a sterling musician, a gorgeous personage. But what they really want is that the people on the other side of the table think their voice is beautiful.

If you can analyze what's good about your voice and write it down, if you can notice clearly the things that need to be fixed, the things that need to be nourished and polished, you have made an important beginning in understanding your strong points and needs as a singer and artist. A singer has to be able to analyze, to be *less critical and more analytical*. Reinforce what you do that's satisfying and write it down. Be a good teacher to yourself! Be positive, be clear, be analytical.

The Group Setting

Begin by describing not only your own voice, but also all other voices you hear: the voices of your colleagues, the voices you hear in performances, the voices on recordings. Write down the various vocal qualities, using adjectives. It's not as easy as it sounds, because it's not a good-or-bad, yes-or-no question. All qualities are distinctive, and many qualities are likable and unlikable. Try to describe a voice so that a friend will know exactly which singer you were talking about. It's a good way of sharpening your ears.

It's also fun to play "drop the needle," (or the compact disc, as it may be now) based on the principle that the better your ear is for other singers, the better it becomes in analyzing your own singing. Have somebody make a tape of the same phrase as sung by different singers. Identify them in as brief a time as possible, so that your ear becomes adept at identifying the distinctive qualities and what makes them distinctive. Don't just use singers who are singing today, but use historical and movie recordings as well. See if you can identify the tenor just from his C during "Che gelida manina" from *La Bohème*. That's really fun.

Now come back to your own singing. Ask yourself, What is the strong point of your technique? Is it your breath, the placement, the flexibility? What's needed? Where are you now? Technique is also not a yes-or-no question.

A group setting is excellent for this type of work. One reason I like to work in a group is because, in that atmosphere, a singer can get an idea of what is so completely and utterly fascinating in opera — opinion. Also, working in a group becomes a good way for a teacher to observe students being observed. The student always working in a room alone does not move easily onto the audition stage.

Group work can provide singers with wonderful reinforcement. It's very beneficial, as well as enjoyable and a great ego booster. By going around the room and asking everybody exactly what they liked about your performance, without going into long, detailed descriptions, you'll begin to hear words that provide positive feedback — enthralling, gorgeous high notes, strong low notes, excellent character portrayal — all kinds of interesting qualities that you may not have realized about your own presentation. This process can be very encouraging, and you may even find it useful to do on an informal basis without a teacher present.

However, in other ways, group work can be very difficult. For one thing, it's scary, especially if you go into it with the attitude, "I could be embarrassed, I could lose face." A better attitude is, "This is my class. I've paid for it. Let's see what I can go home with. I'm going to shop and take home as much as I can."

But for some singers, learning about their voice and themselves, unfortunately, sometimes takes away their confidence, when its purpose is to give you more confidence. As I watch the learning process in young singers, I hear a lot of, "Oh, I didn't do that right, and I don't know that." It sort of whittles you away, instead of making you aware of, "Oh, great, now I know what I don't have and what I need. I'll just go out and get some of that."

Come into a class with questions. "How do I do this?" "What's wrong here?" "How do I make this better?" We should be very demanding of each other. Figure out what you did and how you did it. Don't just say something was boring. Say why. Figure out why something was effective or why it wasn't. *Worry less and work harder!* I find that, as a whole, young opera singers worry too much and find it difficult to work in enough detail. I, myself, used to find ways to worry rather than to work. Once you let yourself be carried away by the enthusiasm for learning a new idea, for finding a new way to do something, you will be infused with a refreshing and revitalizing energy. It will become the only way you want to work.

There should be only one aim: to get the voice, the music and the expression to be more than just right — to be terrific. The opera singer has no safety net.

The Right Questions

The relationship between you and your voice is, of course, very important. After all, your voice is with you twenty-four hours a day. It's important that you be a good parent, a good keeper — that you be responsible for this voice.

We all seem to learn better by being challenged, by having the best demanded of us and by rewarding ourselves for our accomplishments. You don't learn better by being negative. You learn better when the positive action has been reinforced: "The high notes worked pretty well . . ." "I sang an 'ah' vowel once the way my teacher wanted me to . . ." It's easier to do the right thing again, when you know it's the right thing, than to remember not to do the wrong thing. That's much too complicated.

Singing is a very athletic task. Look at how athletes visualize by seeing their entire performance before they do it. Reinforcement of positive action is very important. Today you did this, this and this well. Make an accurate list of what did work. After you sing, it's helpful to sit down and make a few notes about what you did that was good, so it's in your memory and is repeatable.

When your teacher says, This was not good, and this could be better, and the low note wasn't satisfactory, and the G sharp was flat — well, what was good? We tend, in a kind of medical fashion, only to deal with the areas that are not entirely healthy. Ask the questions that will bring out some of your good points and elicit some much-needed positive feedback.

When a singer asks questions like, What did you like, What did I do well today, What did you particularly like about my voice, Did you like the top better than the bottom, it allows someone to answer in a positive fashion. And from that answer, the singer obtains much-needed information.

When you hear, "Not ready for the Metropolitan Opera," or "Not ready for management," this type of answer is very ambiguous, difficult to deal with and certainly does not contribute to a specific learning process. If you're going to the trouble of preparing for an audition, you should be able to at least learn something. It's another good reason for group feedback.

It's Not What They Say

Group work is also a good way to learn from the motto of an old game show, "It's not what you say, it's what you don't say." But whether a singer works in a group or not, it's important to listen to what you're told. People are generally not mean. There's a way of understanding what people say, who says it and why they say it, and understanding also what they *don't* say.

There are lots of clues in what people don't say. What's left out is as important as the comments you actually receive, because, for the most part, no one will say, "You know, your acting was terrible," "Your voice doesn't carry," "Your loud tones wobble." Instead, the singer will hear, "You made it sound very fragile," "You were understated," "Your pianissimos were gorgeous." But you don't really hear about the powerful characterization, the voice that soared over the orchestra, the exquisite high notes.

Part of the reason that singers don't get better faster is that they don't know how to listen, how to interpret their teachers and their coaches. And they don't know how to digest and use information that they do get. It's really very important in the group, audition and career processes to learn to decode what's being said and what's being omitted. Has nobody out of twenty people mentioned your high notes after you sang Queen of the Night? Did not one person mention the quality of your voice, even at least as being interesting? Did nobody say anything about your low notes, your acting, your phrasing, your language? What comment was missing?

If you've just sung Rosina in *Il Barbiere di Siviglia* and you've been told you're stunning and stately, that's fine. But what *didn't* they say? They didn't say you were vivacious, charming and have a lovely, exciting voice, i.e., the qualities usually sought after for a Rosina in a regional house.

After you've sung an aria, if people talk about your acting and your presentation and how convincing you were, this is great. But what didn't they say? Nothing about your voice, your suitability for the role, your musicality?

We are fortunate to live in a time when there is access to live performances, to recordings, to videotapes that will help you understand musical tradition, hear the variety of colors and textures and sizes in voices, and understand your own voice and musicality better as a result. With today's recording technology, there are not as many mistakes left in recordings as there were once upon a time. But don't forget to listen to the older recordings. Yes, the singers are singing in a different musical tradition than is sometimes being performed today — singers tend to be attached to the singers of their own generation — but there's an amazing line there, and you hear that line if you listen to Rosa Ponselle, to Eleanor Steber, and many others. Know historically where you're coming from, absorb what you hear and have the flexibility to learn. And do not judge the great singers on the way they sounded at the end of their careers and write them off as a waste of time! They became famous for a reason. Find out why and learn from these people. It is a waste of time to indulge in musical and vocal snobbery.

Analyze these singers. Who is your favorite and why? And what *didn't* you say? When I ask singers in my classes about their own favorites, their comments are fascinating: "I like so and so. I just heard her, and I absolutely couldn't believe what I was hearing. The voice is incredible." Nothing about the singer's acting, stage presence, interpretation. (With good reason. That particular singer is not a good actor or interpreter, but possesses a remarkably beautiful voice.) It's an excellent exercise for discerning your own strong points and what's being omitted in positive conversation.

One of the best ways to get feedback, when people don't want to tell you what they didn't like — not until you're famous, anyway, at which point they tell you only too often — is to ask people simply what they liked in a performance or, if possible, about an audition. After a competition, when you get the notes back, often the judges look as if they're saying opposite things. But when you look carefully, not really. One judge says, "Pitch insecure." The other judge says, "Vowels not clear." Are they really referring to the same thing? If so, that doesn't mean you have to go home and work on your pitch and your vowels. It means you have to go home and work on the *connection* between your pitch and your vowels. Find the relationship between what people say, what they mean, and what you should do about it.

Become deft with your questions. "Which did you like better?" is a much stronger question than, "What was wrong with my . . ." Use managers, conductors and your own sensitivity to deal with "what was good" and "what was better than." Then you need to deduce, if everybody said you were elegant, sophisticated and warm, that perhaps this is not really Rosina. Maybe you were more the mature Rosina, when she reappears as the Countess in *Le Nozze di Figaro*. It's exciting to see how you can utilize all the comments that are made. They're an important part of your growth for your whole career.

Giving and Receiving Information

None of this analysis is easy. Some of you who are reading this book are probably in that difficult place where you've learned how to sing and are just about ready to go out and perform. You're not yet what you're going to be, but the work toward becoming a professional has started, so you're already somewhat of a professional in your own mind. I'll just say again that the hardest thing a professional singer does, from the Metropolitan Opera to the tiniest studio, is develop the strength of ego and confidence and commitment to go out in front of an audience and be all those things you want to be — a brilliant singer, a vulnerable, dynamic, charismatic actor or actress — only to take a voice lesson and hear, "Now, dear, this wasn't, and this wasn't, and this wasn't."

Lack of defensiveness is important. It allows you to *hear*. One of the biggest hindrances is a defensive shell that, while it keeps you from being devastated, also makes you angry with people who are trying to help you. It can render you unable to be open enough to work and learn.

It's difficult, to say the least, to keep alive that vulnerable part of you that loves the music and not be consumed by outside opinion. Simply try to deal with the *facts*. "Your low notes are really not audible yet" is fact. You can go home and work on this. It's just like saying, "You didn't polish the bottom of the piano," "Your high notes are not round enough in the theater," or "The middle of your voice sounds beautiful, but it doesn't match either the top or the bottom." These are not attacks.

Sometimes it's good to turn outside opinions into observations. "I notice that when you sing in the upper range of your voice, it's much brighter than when you sing in the rest of your voice." No judgement. People can work together very well, if they only ask for observations from each other and resist the impulse to become teachers themselves. We can be most helpful to each other by saying, "I notice when you sing B, you lift up your left foot," or "I noticed your body was much quieter this week."

When you are working in a group or taking your voice lesson or coaching, remember — approval is what you want when you're in front of an audience. In a class or group, approval is nice to have, but it's not really the thing for which you paid money or spent time. You can get approval from your mother for free.

※　　※　　※

Chapter Seven

The Process of
Complete Preparation

If singers would think of each audition as an opportunity to perform, they would perhaps approach an audition with excellent preparation and excitement. I'll go a step further: if each audition were treated as if it were opening night at the Metropolitan Opera or La Scala, I venture to say there would be a different type of preparation and energy than what is often observed.

Let's face it, difficult as it may seem, what auditioners often want is nothing less than a total performance. There are many reasons for this high standard, with the respect we owe our art and the economics of the opera business being the main ones. But also, in most opera house situations, there isn't time for training and retraining, so singers have to demonstrate vocal, musical, linguistic and acting ability and flexibility in the audition. A daunting task, but not impossible.

Creating an Atmosphere

A huge problem singers have is being too general, too *generic* in their approach to an aria. The more professional a person becomes, the more they are able to focus. One way to achieve this focus is to create an atmosphere, both for the aria and also on a particular word, so there is a halo around the piece, as well as specificity around each word and movement. Then you will feel the aria begin to come alive.

If most people were able to do the entire role before they auditioned, that would be an advantage, because an aria, unlike a lied, does not start where it starts! But no one is willing to put on an opera so you can learn an aria.

There are ways around this problem. You can read the score and walk through it while you're listening to a recording. Sit down, get up, pretend it's you singing the role, and see performances with you in your mind's eye up there on stage. Walking through an opera with a recording is inspiring. Here is your table, Mimi. Here is your third act bench, Rodolfo. Here is your bed, Violetta — before you're going to sing "Addio del passato," lie down and go through the words, reading them as the recording plays. Study the text; go through the recording with a libretto and really know what's being said. Have opinions and ideas about what's happening every moment, every hour of the characters' lives. And then you will feel the aria come alive.

If the aria is sung to someone else on the stage, go get someone else. Grab your father, spouse, son, and sing to him "Si, mi chiamano Mimi." Find a handsome guy and tell him, Sit down while I sing you this song. (It could be the beginning of a beautiful friendship!) Rodolfos, go find yourself a girl and sing "Che gelida manina" to her. Feel what it's like to sing these words to another person. Despinas in *Così Fan Tutte*, you're not just singing "In uomini" to yourself, but to two young women, Fiordiligi and

Dorabella. Get your two girlfriends, and explain to them what men are like. For "Come scoglio," Fiordiligi, put two handsome men in front of you with their chests swelling a little bit, and see how it feels to sing that aria. Have them try to touch you every now and again while you're singing it. How's that for inspiration?

For this type of work, I recommend singers get together weekly with a pianist to go through material and sing to each other. You can do that without benefit of a stage director or an orchestra, to give yourself a sense of reality. For those mezzos who sing "Va! laisse couler mes larmes" from *Werther* (a wonderful audition piece, because it shows a lot and it's short), sit, have somebody be your Sophie, hold her in your lap, react to her, stroke her head, hold her face. Talk to her, and watch the aria come alive. It makes an enormous difference.

When you see so many operas, so many performances, it's hard to remember when you're being a transmitter and when you're being a receiver. When you're watching, you can't feel as you do when you're singing. It's a different process, a different energy. The kind of work described above helps you discover that energy.

Thank goodness for modern science. It has invented one of the valuable aids to my musical studies — the "post-it." You can stick one in a score to note almost anything and everything. For a long and repetitive aria like "Ach, ich liebte" from *Die Entführung aus dem Serail,* for instance, decide all the things that are characteristic of this woman: she's tough, fiery. She tells them, Go ahead, cut off my head. Tireless — look at the scales she sings. She's courageous and forthright. Don't use stereotypes — just because you heard somebody sing this aria in a particular way doesn't mean that's the only possibility. Put post-its around the aria indicating changes of thought, changes of emotion, and see how it goes singing the aria like that. Some sections will go well, and some will be absurd. Write "This is the third repeat" or "This is the second time with a variation in minor." It helps you organize your aria in a dramatic way as you figure out what to do emotionally. Use your imagination and instincts. Use your post-its, perhaps in different colors, to keep track of suggestions from different teachers and coaches.

Remember that much of your communication is non-verbal. What you do while the other person is singing is also important. So much of your character in opera develops when you aren't singing. I'll share an exercise given to me by an acting teacher. Write for yourself a silent scenario, one you're going to act without words. Suppose you're to meet someone at a certain time at a certain place. You arrive, but the person doesn't. Or the person is there, but with his or her spouse, when you expected them to be alone. Or you meet a stranger on a train and go home together — that's the kind of situation that can develop enormously. Create any one of a number of sequences. Write them out. Think them out. Act them through without talking. After you've practiced, find a friend and see if they can follow every nuance. Incorporate this into your group work. Ask them to write down what you're doing. Creation of the silent scene itself stretches the mind and the creativity. Then the doing of it stretches you further. Such exercises are valuable particularly for those who do not have access to good acting classes.

Find a good stage director to work with you and stage you through a whole opera, to give you ideas on character, to watch your movements and physical reactions. There are many places today where you can at least be staged in opera scenes. There are also acting groups that will help singers in working on their arias. None of this, however, replaces your own work. It's challenging to see how much you can do on your own.

Finding the Questions

At least twice a month, read through an opera with your

friends, studying it, not necessarily singing it, but translating it and finding out what the questions are. I have heard Maestro Levine suggest this for young students. Learn all about an opera — translate, read, listen — so that when you go to a performance, you are getting questions answered. It's not just watching. You know they have decided to do that, because you know that there's a question about that tenuto. Or this F sharp, is it really sharp or natural? Oh, they sang F natural. What color should I use for this phrase? What is really involved in good Mozart style? Become familiar with the questions and the problems, so that you can begin to find the answers.

If you don't know the arias, how can you really appreciate what Ms. von Stade or Ms. Scotto does? It's up to you to begin your investigation, begin your research into all the elements. Learn the accompaniment. Pretend you only have five minutes to look at a piece of music and see what you can absorb. This is a great exercise for learning well and fast. Your mind is brilliant, and if you force it to, it will remember and absorb a great deal more than you think.

If you want to know what goes on in an aria, see a live performance, as well as listening to a recording. In a live recording or on a live stage, you will hear where the *real* breaths come and the real phrasing. Listen to several recordings — not just one — before learning the music. *Do not learn an aria only by listening to a recording.* Aside from the probability of learning the aria incorrectly, this practice can keep you from forming your own ideas and making your own decisions. As your knowledge of the aria grows, listening to several recordings, on the other hand, can give you valuable information.

Flexibility is one key to successful music preparation. Very seldom has a well-known singer been taught by a single teacher or coach. This enables the singer to learn to do things in a variety of ways. Often, a singer doesn't realize what he or she doesn't know. As a result, you can study for years with a coach or teacher who isn't teaching you. Singers sometimes think there's no more to singing than making a nice sound. A beautiful sound is important, of course, but sooner or later, you have to start showing more than beautiful tone. Make sure you're with the right level of teacher and coach.

A student I know couldn't do something in her voice lesson, and the teacher said to her the next day, "I thought about your problem and I did some research, and I have an idea for something we might try differently today." Most teachers care enough to investigate ways of helping a student further. This is what you should expect from your coaches as well: help. Coaches are not just there to say it's okay or it's not okay. We're on your side. We really are here to help you learn things in a faster, more efficient way.

The Importance of Technique

That's the aria. Now, what about the voice that sings that aria? I once had a singer audition for me with whom I was very impressed, although she had very little on her résumé. I said, "What have you been doing?" Her answer: "I've been learning to sing." You can spend a fortune on your head shots, have a professional-looking résumé, you can jump from coach to coach. But until you get your technique together, until you have a working instrument, it will not be possible to market your singing.

Tailor your technique to your own needs. When you're young, your voice often works 90% of the way on natural instinct and ability, but as you get older, you'll see why you needed that technique. Also, while nervous excitement can help us to exceed our own abilities, nerves can sometimes make us do things worse. Learn how to make something your own, so that it won't disappear and fail you when it's crucial.

Singing is like being a racing car driver. You have four gearshifts and ninety-eight people whizzing around with whom an accident can occur, so you have to know how to shift back and forth. When do I think about my breath? When do I think about the words? When do I think about going slower? Opera singers have to work like athletes, get their breathing right, develop the proper strength to work all the muscles required for singing itself. Think about building the physical strength required, for example, to do a good sword fight in *Romeo et Juliette*, or to get up and down off your knees many times in an opera like *Madama Butterfly*.

Intonation, and by that I mean basic pitch security, is one of the first things you have to control. Until you have good intonation, you should not sing in public (and by that I do not mean classes). Everyone has some intonation problems, but consistently bad intonation is unacceptable.

Projection is another important readiness measurement of singing. Rehearsals and lessons are held in such small rooms that you tend to forget the distances involved in an opera house. Do anything to give yourself an idea of distance, be it singing out the window to the next building or to a tree across the field. Think of having an expansive voice, rather than a bigger one. The voice that's held in won't work; the voice that's released is expanded, resonated and projected. For many, many singers, it's mostly a matter of just getting things out of the way so that the voice can fly freely.

Rent a big hall with a bunch of your friends. Beg or borrow a way into the biggest hall you can find, and spend as much time there as you possibly can. Once upon a time, people even had their voice lessons in a theater and did their coaching on a stage. We can't do that anymore, unfortunately. But by working with your teachers and also working in large spaces and learning how to project, you can get to the honest color of your voice and the real audibility of your sound. There are some voices that feel huge to the singer, but are actually rather inaudible, because they're not produced well. There are also voices that seem small because of incorrect production that, were the production corrected, would project more. All the pushing in the world is not going to help a badly produced voice.

Look for every opportunity to sing with an orchestra, to get the feeling of the buoyancy that the orchestra gives you, that feeling of being able to sing right over it. Again, *without* pushing. Once you're ready to sing professionally — once you have learned to sing — don't let a month go by without performing. I don't only mean in public. When you walk into a voice lesson or coaching session, take those first few minutes to *perform* a piece before getting down to the nitty-gritty of working.

"Staging" an Audition

Now for one of the continual sources of confusion: How much should I move or do in an audition? The rule I learned, the Goldovsky rule, was that any movement which encompassed the space under your arms, anything that was necessary to convey the character and show that you understood the character, was usable. So for the aria "Vissi d'arte" from *Tosca*, movement is not a priority. On the other hand, a Musetta or Juliette who stands stock-still might not be believable. The best criterion, I think, is what the music itself requires, bearing in mind the distinction between *blocking* and *acting*. Sometimes people substitute the blocking for the acting. *They're not the same.*

You don't need to take off your shoes and comb your hair to sing "Ah, fors'e lui" from *La Traviata*. You don't even need to sit down. However, you do need to be contemplative and to project the idea of introspection. For the "Sempre libera" part, the idea of external action is important. You do not need to rip your tiara off and smash a glass against the wall, but you must demonstrate a different kind of energy and movement. Notice what an amazing effect this kind of work has on the release of the voice.

Put yourself in the shoes of the stage director and the opera company administration. "I need to know when I put you on the stage in my opera company that my audience will understand what you're doing. I need to know that you are an actor." Most people's instincts are usually good, if they use them and make precise decisions. "Kind of" and "sort of" don't work.

The more inexperienced the singer, the better it is when you feel free enough to use your hands, your feet, your body. The more common problems of locked knees, locked body and, worst of all, locked breath, can be avoided by focusing, knowledge, involvement and total commitment. Sometimes it helps to work with a stage director who gives workshops. It is astonishing to see how successful this type of work can be for singers.

I've had two interesting learning experiences recently. In one, I went to a riding lesson. "Can you just tell me," I asked, "what you consider the most important thing I can concentrate on?" "Staying on," I was told. Then I took a sailing lesson and was handed the wheel. I said, "What do I do?" "Steer. Don't hit any other boats."

What struck me was the utter simplicity of both these things. You do what you can. Everybody can do something to a different level. The most important thing is to know what your strong points are and use them, play them up. Work on your weaknesses. Bring them up to par. But relish your gift, be it your gorgeous looks, your glorious tones, your sensitive musicianship, your language, your acting, your high notes. It's simple. Just stay on — and don't hit the other boats!

Finding What You Need

I was involved in an opera workshop some time ago where I met a lot of singers who lived outside of major cities. Their big question was, What do I do to learn to sing opera when I get out of college? My question was, Why aren't you learning what you need *in* college? What can be done to alleviate the lack of adequate training caused by teaching music, language and voice for merely a half hour a week? What is the best way to safely get the eighteen-year-old to twenty-three, and the twenty-three-year-old to twenty-six with consistent improvement? Who's responsible for providing what's needed? Teachers, universities and conservatories are all doing everything possible, but *you* need to participate in obtaining what is necessary.

That the majority of twenty-two-year-olds I hear should sing with a bad command of languages is unfortunate. At twenty-two, you can be linguistically knowledgeable. If you're not receiving that training where you are, you have to get it somewhere else. That's not as easy as it sounds. Oshkosh doesn't have as many classes in Italian as Manhattan does. And finding your way into the better schools, where very often the best teachers are reserved for graduate students, is as difficult at times as finding your way into an opera company. I don't know a simple way around this problem, but I know that in the long run, the person responsible for getting the necessary training and knowledge is the singer. There are language tapes, there are videos. That one trip to New York, where you can locate many sources of information, is probably one of the best ways to it. Then take it from there. Figure out what you need and where you can get it. We are all here to help you.

Crossing Cultures and Times

Singing in a foreign language for people who also don't speak the language, singing in a cultural medium that is not our own about worlds that are also not our own, is a difficult proposition. For each year that passes, we move further away from the source of these worlds and the composers' worlds. There was a time once when you could study with the assistant to the assistant of Puccini, with Strauss's student's student. But slowly, slowly, we're losing contact with those ties. Stylistically, things get more difficult, not easier.

On the other hand, we do have better research, we do have better information systems, we do have people who are re-looking into the materials and re-defining what the performance standard of the time was. All the same, it's still culturally an open field.

How do we find a way into the world of the opera in order to be convincing on the stage? The soprano who is playing Tosca can't look as though she's from Omaha, just as the woman who is playing Minnie in *La Fanciulla del West* can't look as though she's from Sicily. The performer's own background and cultural heritage have to be merged with the cultural heritage of the opera in which they are performing. Singers, therefore, have to know the cultural background of each opera in which they perform.

Imagine a young woman from the countryside of France coming to do a production of *Annie Get Your Gun*. What would she have to study? The United States. The old West. The culture, the period, the times, the clothes, the way people moved, the way they spoke. What did it mean when a woman swore? What did it mean when she wore pants? All these infinitesimal outward signs, of movement, of language without words. *La Fanciulla del West* is a wonderful example — an Italian's idea of what the American West was like. *Madama Butterfly* — an Italian's idea of what a Japanese geisha is like. We not only have to understand the Japanese culture, but we have to understand the Italian *idea* of Japanese culture. In *Carmen*, the French idea of a Spanish woman is very different from a Spaniard's idea of a Spanish woman. Or a German's idea.

I want to draw your attention to a review written in 1929 in the *Boston Sunday Post* about Hizi Koyke, a very famous Japanese soprano: "It is safe to say that a performance of Puccini's *Madame Butterfly* more moving than that given by the Boston Grand Opera Company has never been offered to a Boston audience. That a singer of Japanese blood would act the role of Butterfly is a point that scarcely needs laboring. No western soprano can possibly bring complete illusion." What this singer gave the role was something inherent in her blood, her background, her tradition. An Italian singing Butterfly would bring something inherent in *her* blood, her background and her tradition to Puccini's music. If you're not of the background called for by a particular role, it takes a great deal of study and hard work to arrive at what is necessary. Unfortunately, born and bred American singers are faced with a greater challenge, with the majority of operas being written by foreign composers about people in foreign lands. And all singers are challenged when setting out to sing operas set in historical times.

This cultural intuition, the ability to look back through the years at the mind and mores of a society, is very important to the person who wishes to fit into an opera, a period, a time. Our imagination and our knowledge have to go hand in hand. All the books that we can read, all the pictures we can find, all the movies we can see that stimulate our imagination and visualization, are essential to finding our way into these worlds.

I once tried to do a scene from *Susanna* with some Italian singers who wanted to sing in English. Trying to explain the Baptist preacher, Reverend Blitch, to a Sicilian Catholic was a lesson in cross-cultural teaching. Never mind Baby Doe and the "seelver" mine. It all sounds very funny until you remember that *you* have to make a *living* singing in *their* culture, and most of you don't know about it. Are you any more familiar with their culture than they are with ours? Those Italian singers can spend the rest of their lives having wonderful careers and never go near an American opera. So can you, maybe. But you'll probably have to go near the Italian ones, not to mention the German and French ones. You have to study how to react the way the Italians reacted, the way the French reacted throughout history. When Puccini wrote Musetta, it was an Italian idea of how a French woman behaved. What is the difference between Mozart when he writes in German and Mozart when he writes in Italian? The Italian operas are often about who's trying to get whom into whose bed for what reason. In the German operas, you have more metaphysical libretti, such as *Die Zauberflöte*, essentially about philosophy and ideas. There is a big difference between German and Italian, between metaphysical and physical operas.

The very best course is to go into these countries and absorb the atmosphere, the history, the culture. There's nothing like being in Florence, listening to the stories, reading Dante and the literature and history books of that period when preparing *Gianni Schicch*i. Later, the sight of *bella Firenze* coming to your mind as you sing about it is most inspiring.

Go and live in other cultures. One of the gorgeous things about America is that you can find centers of any culture you want, especially in the larger cities. See if you can find a family from Italy, a family from France. If you're still in college, living abroad as part of your college program is one of the wisest investments you can make. To acquire a spoken, reading acquaintanceship with the language, with the country, with the history, with living history, are invaluable. It's as though you were becoming a pantomimist, learning the language of other people, other nations, other hands. Many of us have body language typical of Canadians, Americans, Mexicans, which doesn't happen to look particularly effective as Violetta in *La Traviata*. Not that the language of *Traviata* is even available to us today, but certainly the Italian idea of a French girl of this period and this background is available to our imagination.

Do you need to spend the day in a Carmelite monastery if you're going to do the *Dialogue des Carmelites*? No, but a day passed in absolute silence and prayer surely can't hurt, and you will come to that opera with something quite different if you have given yourself some visual and emotional reality. Find every book that you can to bring to life the period of historical struggle between Italy, Germany and Austria. Know the whole Austro-Hungarian influence on music and society, down to how much a woman could own and what her rights were, all of which has so much to do with the way women are presented in opera. What was going on in the world when these operas were written is so important. Without that, the characters really don't assume their third dimension.

There was a different kind of emotionalism in the 1700s. People kept a lot more emotion inside. In the later 1800s, they were more outgoing (but still not like the 1990s). There is the whole *verismo* school that stopped writing about what happened to the king and queen when they met in the evening, but started talking instead about the little girl from the village who had real problems! You have a whole new set of people appearing in opera then, and this needs to be studied. Look at the birth and death dates of the composer, and write down a few other things, such as who else was alive and what was going on politically, events from that period which make the era real for you. A great sourcebook for this is *Timetables of History* by Bernard Grun.

It's interesting when you see somebody playing Don Giovanni to notice that he's always standing with his leg turned out. Knowing the reason why — women looked at a man's calf in those days — helps it make sense. Go and look at the paintings of the period. All the men had their legs turned out and their arms up. Notice all the frills and lace they wore, and think of the mentality that went along with how they looked and how they dressed.

Investigate other art forms. Paintings in museums are some of the best information sources. Also see how the great performers of other times have approached these periods and styles in history. Acting styles change, yes; talent does not. The great acting styles have been documented and are available to be seen, in the same way that dancers study other dancers, handing down a tradition of style, leaving the best and discarding what is no longer useful.

Ultimately, you are best suited to the music your voice and personality feel most comfortable performing. We in this country do have a style of opera all our own, and you may find that you're really suited for that style vocally, temperamentally and emotionally. If so, go with it. This may be the music that makes you hirable. If you don't like modern music, but your voice is suited for it, your temperament is suited for it, your style is suited for it — do it anyway. You'll grow to love it. There's nothing like being successful for learning to love something!

%   %   %

Chapter Eight

For the College Student

When I look at the regional competitions, I frequently see many very good singers coming from the same areas. They may not always win, but there are often four, five, eight terrific singers from these same regions and cities consistently. I used to think, What is it? The water? Strangely enough, there are other cities, sometimes bigger, where the number of good singers is not consistent, and it is interesting to speculate on what is functioning and what is not.

Every college, every music school, is trying to offer the very best to their students. We know, however, that there are not only the students to satisfy, but the public, the benefactors, the board and the faculty.

Each of these factions has the best interests of the students at heart. But in the complexity of the college/music school system, the individual student may not always feel that way. I travel to many schools to teach, and the differences are just amazing. The teachers who believe that the process is important seem to really produce the singers who function the best in the world of opera.

Those who only emphasize a final performance and personal allegiance (not loyalty, but neurotic allegiance) tend *not* to produce great singers, it seems.

Caught in the Middle

Occasionally, in a school setting (and this is by no means the rule), little tugs of war develop. It's like the horseracing in Siena once upon a time — each squadron has its backers. It's not abnormal, but taken to an extreme point, it can be detrimental to the young singer who doesn't know how to handle the situation. Like the child who's mystified because his or her parents argue with each other, it tends to make the child insecure. Students don't understand that fundamentally, there's respect among all these factions, and that perhaps these teachers essentially have the same goals. But the bickering that can go on between adjacent voice teachers, between coach and voice teacher, between the head of the opera workshop and voice teachers — all these people saying, This way, This one, Why not that, Why not this, each person struggling for the sunlight, can be confusing for the student caught in the middle.

In all teaching situations anywhere, there is a kind of prize for having the most talented singers in your studio, workshop or program, which sometimes only happens because we teachers were lucky enough to have them a particular year. In some seasons, two or three or four of my students win competitions, some seasons, none. And I don't think how intelligent or how perceptive I've been that year matters. Frankly, to be able to get somebody who is an unsophisticated beginner to the point of being moderately good is a much more difficult teaching task than taking somebody who's already terrific and helping them become fantastic. All too often, young singers find that the best teachers are usually available only to graduate students or the very best singers. The younger student, the least experienced person vocally, at times is studying with the least experienced teacher. This can make the growing process difficult, especially if a student has serious vocal problems. Face the problem and deal with it as straightforwardly as you can.

Another issue that can deeply affect a student in the college setting is a situation where the young head of the opera workshop or the coach is not particularly dedicated to that institution or to the students, but rather, is just starting out in the opera business and trying to make a career himself. We understand his ambition, but it makes, of course, for different energies. An opera director with an eye on New York is not very interested in teaching the young and inexperienced, but can tend, rather, to favor casting the naturally gifted or the graduate student — a more finished product. That kind of opera director is not able to really be involved in the process of nurturing. The person who is trying to establish a career can sometimes leave a young, inexperienced singer feeling lost and inadequate. This can be devastating for a talented student who needs to be *taught* in order to have their abilities brought to the surface. Fortunately, this is a situation we don't come across very often. It is the exception, not the rule.

Your college years are the time when you are least prepared and least able to handle power struggles and stand up for yourself. Finding somebody who can help you decode what you are listening to, who is responsible for what, what your responsibilities are, and how best to handle an uncomfortable and tense situation, is necessary. Find someone out in the professional world and talk to them, perhaps someone teaching in your institution. You'll calm down. Generally, the people who are working, or who have worked, are very good at making sense of a situation and are able to stay out of these little nitty-grittys. There is always someone like that available. Always. Go and find the person who can help.

Even though these problems occur, unhappily, at a fragile time in your life when you're least equipped to deal with them, as much as you can, see this kind of situation as something that has to do with them, not you, and understand it as a microcosm of what might happen in the real world. Learn how to handle the problem, and remind yourself that the college world and the professional world are different. There's much less of this type of situation out in the real world. I guess we professionals have our eye on a bigger value, like the composer and the performance. Also, the real world isn't quite so small and insulated.

Loyalty

Our first loyalty is to ourselves and our music. But let's define loyalty. A teacher who has really stood by you and helped you absolutely deserves recognition and should not be forgotten. I once found it heartbreaking — I find it amusing now — to have helped a singer find a characterization for a role, or helped with finding a voice teacher, and then hear them say to a member of the audience after a successful performance, "Well, it just kind of happened." When a singer gets a great review on incredible, innate musicality after hours and hours of work, a little murmured word of, "I think you helped, thanks," is really nice. This kind of loyalty we all need. If in twenty lessons a voice teacher gives a singer a beautiful high C, this is not something to be looked at lightly. If a program notes, "Costumes by So and So, Make-up by So and So," why not, "High C by So and So?" A little card that reads, "Sang great high C last night, thanks," is the breath of life to people who teach. Don't forget that, in a school setting or anywhere else. It's our applause.

However, that's not the kind of loyalty I'm talking about. In a school setting, you may run into a teacher and a coach who may not agree, an opera workshop director who wants you in one kind of repertoire, a teacher who disagrees with your assigned coach, and you may be asked to choose. I'll give just a small example. A music school student I know worked on "Come scoglio" with her coach, took it into her voice teacher and was told the entire recitative was incorrectly coached. The teacher became so angry that she dragged the student into the coach's studio and demanded an explanation. The coach claimed he hadn't taught the recitative the way the student was singing it, which made the student look and feel rather foolish. The voice teacher was the most powerful in the school, and the coach, a very young and ambitious man, didn't feel he was in a position to disagree with her. But it left the student embarrassed and shattered. It's far better when we leave the drama for the stage!

Ego — Yours and Others

The skill that it takes to understand who you are and what you're dealing with is a real indicator of how you're going to be able to deal with the business end of opera, as opposed to the music. It's useless to say, "I really only know how to deal with music," because you *have* to deal with everything else.

In life, there are directors, conductors, coaches, voice teachers, a myriad of people who may be difficult for you to get along with; but what they have to offer is so valuable, that dealing with the difficulty is worth it. However, there is no need to play into what is neurotic. If the school is really taking away your spirit and your confidence, move. You say, Oh, how can I move, where can I go? There's a feeling among young students very often that this is the only voice teacher in the school I want to work with, that only this school has a good opera department. But there's always another place. If not, the cost can be very great. It can result in a lost voice — not a voice lost by illness, but by lack of confidence and self-esteem. Voices are very sensitive to emotional trauma.

There are many teachers who have their egos well in hand and who don't need to carve a piece of the student's ego to replace their own. If you find yourself in an uncomfortable situation, and you are learning more than you could learn in any other situation, relax and live with it. It will be over soon. If you are making vocal, musical, theatrical progress beyond your wildest dreams, stick it out. But if you hear that the tapes from this month are worse than your audition tape, that your voice is closing down, your personality is closing down, you're not learning another piece of music, you don't want to practice, you don't want to study — then maybe you're in the wrong place. And let's face it — maybe a place less famous, smaller, in a slightly smaller city is the place for you. Perhaps a place a trifle less mainstream. Maybe your career is not going to be at the Met, Covent Garden or La Scala. Maybe your career is going to be Caracas, Sydney, Toronto, Marseilles and Florence, or perhaps even less mainstream than those. What a wonderful career that is! Everybody doesn't have to live on Fifth Avenue, and everybody doesn't have to go to a huge music school in a large city.

Finding Your Options

And do you know what? A degree is important, of course, and I would be the last person to negate its benefits, but it's also possible not to go to music school and still have a career. For the amount of money that it takes to go to most schools, if you're the kind of person who does not need an externally structured organization, you can structure your own program. Who's to say you can't come to New York, have two hours of music theory with a very good teacher, two hours of language a day, a voice lesson three times a week instead of two half-hours, a movement class, a coaching session twice a week and belong to a small opera workshop for the same dollars? You won't have the privilege of saying, "I graduated from such and such" and all the future benefits a degree can bring, but on the other hand, there is no benefit from attending a school where you can't learn anything or participate. But I would say the type of person who can embark on their own without the structure of a college is not the norm. The usual route is a music school or college degree, followed perhaps by graduate work. This is very necessary if teaching will be any part of your career, since you cannot teach without a degree.

Remember, you *always* have options. Never allow yourself to believe that you don't, that this is the *only* school, the *only* teacher. There is no *only* anything, except your voice and your soul, and you have to hold onto those at all costs.

※ ※ ※

Chapter Nine

When to Audition — And Where

The decision of whether or not you're ready for an audition is something to be worked out within yourself, and with teachers and coaches. The condition of your voice, repertoire, nervous system, all enter into the decision. If you're in the throes of working out a major technical problem, it's generally not a good time to go out and audition. If you're changing your repertoire, voice type or teacher, it's not a good time either. A class or even an informal grouping with friends is invaluable at this point, to give you a chance to try out new pieces.

Part of your decision to audition depends on the audition itself. For the beginning singer, opera companies that have apprentice programs can be a marvelous training ground and a good foot in the door. These auditions are certainly available and, while very competitive, offer opportunities to perform and learn.

Age "Requirements"

But alas, the beginning singer is sometimes not a young singer by the standards of some of these apprentice programs. The age issue, to speak frankly, is one of the more difficult issues to deal with in opera. On the other hand, take heart, because the older a singer is, the more stable he or she is likely to be, and there are still many opportunities available.

There is the usual American "interesting information" about age (i.e., it seems to be everyone's business), as there is the European tradition of "interesting information" about one's salary. Europeans don't seem to have quite the same trouble with age that we do. However, part of the age problem is practical. At a certain age, there are fewer years left for the growth cycle necessary to manage a career and make it work. When, for example, a voice peaks between thirty-five and forty-three, you want to be in the midst of a career at that time.

We need to understand that opera singers are people first and have lives outside their careers that can detour them. Sometimes, a woman will decide between twenty-four and twenty-eight to have her children, and so at twenty-nine, she is just beginning her studies, which at thirty-three really puts her in a good position. But she's past the limit for a lot of competitions. And nature itself can often dictate the timing of one's career. Men's voices are often a bit more difficult to excavate and can take a little longer to develop. By the time the high baritone discovers he is a tenor, he may find himself out of the running for many apprentice programs or competitions.

If you ignore the age issue, fine. Many people are very crafty at not revealing their age. But if proof of age is needed, it's really rather useless to think that you can avoid the question. Don't worry. If all your vocal, musical and dramatic abilities are polished, age won't really matter in the long run. If you don't fit in one place, you'll find some place where you do. There are still competitions which are either age-free or where the age limit is wide. And if that doesn't work, there are European competitions that sometimes have no age limit. There are many more competitions and auditions than you might think — all you have to do is look in the library and read all the opera magazines and publications. If there are no competitions in your area, see if you can get an organization to sponsor one; make the prize a trip to New York. Find judges in the local music schools. Be innovative and resourceful.

Competitions vs. Auditions

Is there anything different about a competition as opposed to a regular audition? Yes, in many ways. A competition has a broader aspect. It is often a way to see what the future will be. There are many kinds of people in a competition. They usually fall into two categories: those who are ready to go on and actively work on their career, and those who are showing potential. Contest judges look for a substantial and unique talent. Whether it's already refined and sophisticated or still in raw form, it has to be special.

Potential is not as much a part of an audition for a role in an opera company. For a job, you have to show actuality, which is one of the reasons why it's valuable if you can sing an aria from the opera for which you're auditioning. If you don't know one and don't feel you can prepare adequately in time for the audition or find an appropriate substitution from your current repertoire, perhaps this is an audition you should skip.

Management Auditions

I've heard lots of managers say you can only be managed when there's something to manage. You can only start building a career when it's possible to have a career. There is a point before which it's foolish to expect to have one. Just because you recently graduated from college doesn't mean you absolutely must have a manager today. Just because you've had your two hundredth voice lesson doesn't mean you now need a manager.

The time to sing for a manager is when you think you have something that's salable. So maybe you're not quite ready all the way; maybe your pianissimo, diminuendo, crescendo and sforzando are not quite perfect. However, you do a great Susanna, you look right, your language is right, you know how to do recitatives, you can move around the stage with ease, you know how to integrate with other singers well and your sense of ensemble singing is excellent. Let's not stay home until the high C, crescendo, diminuendo are absolute perfection!

It's appropriate to demonstrate to a manager where you are now and where you will be in two or three years. The manager should know what your future might include — not only your future in opera, but your future in vocal symphonic music, sacred music, oratorio and concert. It doesn't hurt for a manager to see that a singer has future engagements when the singer comes in to audition. Future contracts tell a manager something about the singer's salability. You may say, Well, it is the manager's job to get me work! This is true in part, but your responsibility for keeping an ear to the ground and doing all the things necessary to gain employment do not end when you sign a contract with a manager. Learning to work with a manager is a special kind of challenge. It takes your cooperation, participation and the same hard work that all good relationships require.

Which Auditions to Take

A wonderful manager told me that a singer should work for

one or more of the following: joy, learning, prestige, money and experience. I found this has served me as a quick guideline in deciding which auditions to attend and in understanding what opportunities I wanted and why.

Mezzo-sopranos, what kinds of roles should you take? The smaller roles now, the bigger roles later? The bigger roles in smaller places, the smaller roles in bigger places? Mezzos, basses and baritones especially face these kinds of decisions often. You can be hired for a wonderful smaller role, and I would suggest that you do so when the opportunity for learning is high. If you're offered Borsa in *Rigoletto* and the tenor in the opera is Alfredo Kraus or Carlo Bergonzi, take it! If you're going to be hired to do Borsa and the conductor and director are inexperienced and the soprano sings out of tune, you might consider whether this is a real opportunity for you or not. If you have a chance to do Frasquita or Mercedes with a great Carmen, a wonderful Micaela, good costumes and good surroundings, that experience can be exhilarating, eye-opening and a step up in your growth.

Try to resist the audition that is going to lead you to a job of little value, i.e., one where there will be inadequate rehearsal or musical and dramatic preparation. A danger inherent in auditioning for that type of situation is that you could get the job. Then what do you do? You're in for an experience which will unlearn for you. I think the temptation is so great just to get on your feet and sing a role that singers often don't think about the consequences. But if that has to be the situation, you need to spend the most amount of time and the most amount of money in the most professional preparation that you can, along with thorough coaching. Find a great singer who did the role a hundred times, and prepare yourself as though it were your world debut at the Met. If you do that, then the situation is not quite such a detrimental one. But usually — and it's very hard to see in the beginning — when you start in an atmosphere of compromise, you very soon learn how to compromise yourself. The compromising becomes easier and easier, and musical standards begin to slip. Your reputation suffers, and the mention of your name is accompanied with, "Yes, they're good enough for the circuit," or "Well, a good regional singer." Somehow, the opportunity to make an upward move is all of a sudden not yours anymore. "No, we don't want to listen to him. He's routine." Or to quote someone I heard after an audition, "Well, we were very underwhelmed." Your musical integrity is so very important, it's worth a great deal not to have to compromise your standards of preparation.

On the other hand, I know some singers who have outwaited their chances by waiting until total perfection has set in. This is usually accompanied by advanced age and a passing parade. When you feel you're in the ballpark of professional, go. If you want to sing for these people at all costs and don't care about this particular job, you can go and sing an aria for them that has nothing to do with what they're doing, but will just give them information about you as a singer, who you are and what you do. Often a screening audition for a theater can be like that — a great opportunity to be heard and for the auditioners to learn who you are, what kind of material you have and what a fine artist you are.

The Re-Audition

What does one do, for instance, in the case of an apprentice program, competition or theater for which you sang last year and are refused another audition, even though you've improved? My personal feeling is that we forget how fast singers change and that we do need to hear and re-hear young singers often. But, yes, there are circumstances like that in which it is difficult to be re-heard. The reason is usually the necessity of hearing a great number of singers in a short amount of time, so time is reserved for people not yet heard. Find out which companies do this by talking to your friends and coaches, and consider staying away from those auditions. Stay away from them until you're pretty sure that most of the comments you're getting back are positive. "Professional." "Sounds great, look great." At the least, you want your report to come back and say, "Extraordinarily well prepared, but we don't think the voice is ready yet." This can get you another audition. "Voice not ready, preparation not interesting" is perhaps not the type of thing that can win you another audition. Try a few auditions, and see what kind of feedback you're getting. Sing for some coaches, directors, conductors and get some feedback to guide you in timing your auditions.

Critiques and Their Value

If the audition you attended isn't one where you have access to a critique, it can be useful to try to solicit their comments. Granted, people are busy, but we are totally aware of where the talent is coming from, and without young talent, opera has no future. So, you can ask, In what area do you think I need to grow before I audition for you again? Then use that when you write for the next audition: "I so much appreciated your remarks, and I think in this area, according to Mr. So and So, So and So and So and So," (which are of course recognized names that they will trust) "my accomplishments in the past two years have been notable." This approach is certainly worth a try and may win you another hearing. Most people involved in opera are, at the risk of going out on a limb, relatively reasonable.

There are some people for whom it is useless to audition. If someone really believes you can never grow as a singer, never can sing a certain role, let the situation go, and don't pursue that particular audition route. We often get trapped into the "conquer the person" syndrome, which can be needlessly discouraging. You can sing for other people.

The Importance of Research

Read all the opera magazines to get an idea of what kinds of singers are being hired and where. You will, in all probability, not be discovered in a coffee shop or a practice room, so you must be resourceful. Study, read and be familiar with all the journals about our business. And remember, if someone is choosing between two people of equal talent, they will, in all likelihood, choose the one they know and have experience with. Many times, when an opera company is going to hire somebody they don't know, it will often be for a role like Micaela and Musetta. These are showy roles, but the success of the entire opera does not hang on them. The same is true of Pinkerton. On the other hand, these roles certainly can demonstrate the possibilities a singer has. There are other roles like this, of course, and it is important to think along these lines.

It helps to take a look at the people hired by apprentice programs and use your peer groups to study yourself accurately. Avoid saying, "Oh, he's better than me," or "I'm better than he is. I don't know why they hired him." Try to figure out why they hired him when they had every opportunity to hire you. What were they looking for? Don't leave personal preference out of the equation; judging voices is a very subjective thing. Whatever you do, don't get into the "I'm-as-good-as-Pavarotti-why-don't-they-hire-me" syndrome. It ruins your spirit and has no effect on the job market.

It's not a bad idea to know the names and positions of the people involved in opera in different companies across the country. How nice to be introduced to Mr. So-and-So and know what he just sang or conducted! Businessmen make these personal investments regularly, and you, too, should know your own profession.

Each audition presents a special circumstance and, best of all, a special opportunity. Make your decisions wisely, with good advice, and if your voice has a 90 percent chance of working — go! Audition!

❦   ❦   ❦

Chapter Ten

The Audition

An audition is really a performance. There is not one rule for performing and another for auditioning — all we want you to do is share yourself musically and emotionally. It is not a test, and we are not a jury. It's an opportunity to let people know who you are, what your talent is like, what your strengths are, and what is wonderful about you. Like a blind date, the idea may not be fun, but the actual experience can be interesting and satisfying.

Singers very often lose sight of the fact that their talents are needed and wanted; that in fact, the auditioners are there to see *them*. Singers are the lifeblood of this business, and without them, opera conductors, coaches, prompters and opera directors can't do their jobs or the music that we all love. As a singer matures and has gone the audition route many times, he or she often begins to feel that they are wasting their energy and that their work is not respected by the listeners. A certain resentment can set in, which results in a poor attitude, poor cooperation, poor singing and poor preparation. All of which leads to lack of employment, and the vicious circle has begun.

Auditioning is part of your lives. If it doesn't work out, you do it again. It's relatively costly, but not more costly than giving up your career. Until you're out of that unfortunate position of having to audition, I don't know what else you can do. It's a buyer's market, after all. If you needed to sell your home, you wouldn't think twice about people wanting to see the house early in the morning. It's never too much trouble. If you want to sublet your apartment, you show it to whomever has credentials to rent it. Some people come four times; some don't show up. It's part of the game. And guess what? If you don't like it, you take your house off the market.

Competition judges, opera company administrators, conductors and managers are all waiting to discover the next great singer. I promise you, they will not let a great singer get away from them. Often, it's the singers who are close, but not quite there who sometimes slip away. Sheer numbers of singers is frequently the reason. The people who are listening may have been there since ten o'clock in the morning, and you may be singer number 486. If you are sensational, if you really deliver, the auditioners will be engaged and grateful. Believe me. But if you come in and are protective, not ready to display your talent, unwilling to communicate, not prepared to give everything you have, the people who have been sitting still since early morning can fall into a kind of tedium, hard as they try to fight it. These people want something. They love singing and singers. They are excited about great potential, as well as the talent that's ready to go. They're hungry for something. Give it to them.

Remember that it's not only the beginning singer who has to audition. As you develop, you will find that your voice has grown and changed, and your repertoire has also changed. In the middle of your career, you may find that you're singing different music or should be singing different music than you were before. And so there is a re-auditioning for the opera company. Or should I say, there is the re-information process.

Showing Who You Are

I think the word "audition" is a misnomer. Let's call it an "info-dition" instead. You're making yourself available to be heard, and you're giving people information about yourself, information that they need and want. I can't think of a single circumstance where you don't want people to know about you, if you're ready.

Yet sometimes singers act as if they don't want auditioners to know anything at all about them. I've heard so many auditions of singers who were amazingly ill-prepared, with no more idea of style than the man in the moon, no differentiation in style between Mozart and Mascagni. No attempt to bring us a display of their vocal qualities or abilities — great crescendo, warm low notes, a gorgeous silvery delicate quality, for instance — by choosing the right kind of music. Languages all over the place. When comments are made about these problems, it's easy to say, "Yes, yes, I know that, but I didn't have time," or "My coach wasn't available."

So be sure of the strength of your commitment and have a good attitude. Follow it up with some really solid preparation, and most of all with some excitement.

How to Prepare

Now let's take a look at what faces you, not only at the audition, but also before it.

You've got to know yourself. I cannot emphasize this enough. Some people can't work a full day and then do an audition, and if you're one of those people, you need to take the day off. Some people need peace and quiet on audition day, others prefer to be more social. Some people find a coaching on the day of an audition useful, some find it better the day before. Some shouldn't coach for several days before, because for them, the "improvements" are confusing. There are those who want to rehearse with their accompanist right before the audition. Find out what works best for you and do that.

I want to remind you that it is crucial to rehearse. Accompanists are part of the music, and rehearsal is very important to make the partnership work. Accompanists should want to rehearse under most circumstances, and if they don't, I suggest you find another one.

This is only a part of good, solid preparation, the kind that's going to make you feel great as you walk out on stage. The preparation continues with the flattering dress or suit that doesn't upstage you, the comfortable (shined!) shoes you've had on before, the slip that doesn't cling to you (never go to an audition without your declinger). Bring one little package that can hold declinger, special vitamin pills, water, lucky charm, a spritzer bottle of water, if only to keep the air in front of you moist. After all, if the Met can spray the stage for five full minutes before a singer walks out on it, you can certainly spray the air in front of you. Spray a little on your handkerchief, and breathe the humidity. Don't allow yourself to get dry. Laryngologists recommend that for singers, especially on performance days, the normal "eight glasses of water" can be added to, even doubled.

Spend time learning how to deal with your nerves. Do you need to sit quietly in a corner or distract yourself with some light conversation? Do you need to don headphones and listen to a meditation tape or some soothing music? Read a book? Whatever you do, keep your breaths deep and calm, especially as you approach the stage.

We have many remedies for bad nerves nowadays: biofeedback, imagery, massage, the advantages of so much knowledge about exercise. Find what helps you handle your nerves and use it. Nervousness is, at times, unavoidable, and you have to learn to sing through a nervous state, even translate it into a kind of excitement, but paralytic nervousness is not normal. Be assured that you can discover a way to handle it, though you may have to search a little harder for the answer than most.

The process of waiting, sometimes a long time when the audition is running late, can be very difficult. You may need to run into the ladies' or men's room or go outside and do a few scales to keep your voice warmed up. Know when you need to "rev up" ahead of time before singing a piece and how you have to vocalize. Again, it's a question of knowing what your voice requires.

The Audition

Finally, your name is called.

For a consequential audition, be sure you have a pianist you know and trust. If you're not from the city where you're auditioning, it's a good idea to coach with someone when you get there, who will then either play for you or help you find an accompanist. Names of coaches can be obtained from the opera companies in that city or from your friends. If you use an accompanist provided by the listeners, be sure that you know your tempi and that you can communicate them to the pianist by being a strong leader.

Assuming you have brought your own accompanist, it's advisable to talk to your pianist in advance and plan your entrance. This is crucial, so that one of you is not impaled on the point of the piano, so that the the pianist doesn't try to walk behind the singer as the singer hugs the nook of the piano. I've seen both approaches. It's your audition, so know what you're doing. It's best not to leave it up to the pianist. As you walk out, hold your head up and enjoy the moment (or at least look like it). It's what you've worked for — make your entrance!

Sometimes you're in a strange city and haven't brought your own accompanist, or your accompanist is ill, or your accompanist is also playing for the person right before you and is already on stage. The point is, if you must give the accompanist your music on stage, it's better to go to the upstage side of the piano. If you go downstage, it's a somewhat less pretty picture, especially if you turn your back to the judges and lean over to show the accompanist a cut in the music. The five pounds you've wanted to lose is there for all the world to see. And please, please, make sure your music is in good shape for the accompanist to read. Cuts should be clearly marked or covered with paper (if we can't see it, we won't play it). Never hand a pianist anything with loose staples. Do not use shiny covers on your music which will reflect the light and leave you singing a cappella.

It's often quite a revelation in my classes for students to hear from other students how they come across when they give their name and announce their aria: aggressive, fearful, shy, angry. It also comes as a revelation that this introduction has to be rehearsed and announced into a tape recorder and in front of a mirror, so that you can see yourself and hear yourself. These steps are necessary, because inaudibility can be a big problem when singers announce themselves, even with all that projection training. Also, singers' innermost thoughts are often very apparent, and some of them are better left off their faces. And if this opening is not prepared, it's easy to trip over the name of the composer or title of the aria. Your pronunciation of the title of the aria and the opera is just as important when you speak as when you sing. Decide ahead of time what language you are using for the title of the opera; for instance, "I will sing 'Deh vieni, non tardar' from *The Marriage of Figaro* (or *Le Nozze di Figaro*)." It's also a gracious gesture to announce the name of your accompanist, who is, after all, a partner in your audition. But you can remain facing out as you do so.

These first minutes are your minutes. I loved listening to the wonderful soprano, Judith Raskin, teach singers to say, instead of "My name is . . ." to say "I am . . ." — "I am Jane Smith." A small, but unique difference.

What Auditioners Look For

What is the first thing auditioners write about, generally? Quality of voice. This is not a yes-or-no question, since quality is difficult to pinpoint, but this generally refers to the first reaction the listener has to the sound of your voice.

Technical strengths are important on the audition sheet: what your breath control is like, evenness of registers, command of high notes, control of coloratura, smooth transitions in the voice, vocal attacks and releases, control — all the interesting details that technique encompasses. Size of voice, which is relative to the size of the theater and may sound different to the singer than it does to the listeners, is important only because we need to know what roles to fit it to. We do about twice as many operas for lyric voices as we do for spinto or dramatic.

The next item on the audition sheet will generally concern the singer's skills, and this is a place where singers can excel, always: language, musicality, style, musicianship, intonation, phrasing.

There's one other little thing that is added later, if auditioners are interested in hiring you. Because we have faxes and such instant communication, people are able call an opera company where the singer has worked and ask about their spirit of cooperation, their temperament, how he or she got along with others. This business has the biggest information exchange after Wall Street. Summer programs are often your first experience with the pleasures and difficulties of working together with a group of your fellow artists. Although it's sometimes difficult even to deal with ourselves in stressful performance-oriented, learning-oriented situations, let alone dealing with twenty or thirty other singers, keep in mind that these situations are where your reputation is established.

Preparation Errors

Let's look at some problems made in auditions that can easily be avoided.

It's obvious to a judge when something hasn't been well coached. The first and most critical thing is that you be on top of your music. If you're asked to list five arias and, out of desperation, you've added a fifth that's not really ready and you just know they aren't going to ask for it, Murphy's law will then go into effect. Nine times out of ten, that's the one they'll ask for.

The second thing is, it does not make people comfortable to think that they will have to present a singer who may appear nervous and flustered. That reads badly. They can't afford that, and neither can you. Many people say, "I do better on stage than I do in an audition situation." But you have to be as comfortable in an audition as in a performance. In most cases, that "I do better" statement is untrue. However, it may be true in the case of a singer who needs to be totally involved with the stage, costumes and character, and who may need weeks of preparation. If this is your situation, then remember to make each aria a total performance internally. Be so focused that you can put that over. There's a relationship between preparedness and ease. Anxiety tends to be less of an issue if you know what you're doing. If you're not confident, remember the next most important thing — fake it. Pretend. Use your imagination. Create. Remember every good and glowing comment you ever heard about your singing, and keep those thoughts going in your mind.

What would it be like if I said to you, You're the greatest

Mozart singer I ever heard? What if you had a big contract to sing this piece somewhere? What would you do if you were going to make the first few bars thrilling? Or if you were singing for these people not as an unknown, but as a tremendous diva just back from a European tour, back singing for her home opera company? Find what works for you and use it. There are several books to help teach you to keep your mind where it will help you the most. Take a look at *The Inner Game of Tennis* and *Soprano on Her Head*. If "make-believe" and "let's pretend" will give you a feeling of zooming confidence, use them.

An insecure singer can be helped by taking a moment before starting to sing. Do you take the time to prepare yourself, to feel focused, to feel in character? A true artist works toward being fully grounded. Work toward that. Don't rush your moments! And fill them with atmosphere. Those moments include the introduction. Don't just wait for the piano to finish so you can sing.

The people listening need to feel and hear the sound, to see a gesture completed, musical or otherwise. Because, for instance, in "Caro nome" from *Rigoletto*, cadenzas have been added, you have to time them out yourself so they are satisfying. Don't rush your cadenzas and jump off your high notes.

Many singers have a tendency, when they audition, to want to make a big sound rather than a beautiful one. Singers often want to want to show that they have big voices. If you have one, don't worry. The judges will be able to tell. If you don't, all the screaming in the world won't give you one. Forget about going out there and impressing people with size. Forget about the movies you've seen where the producer stands up after an audition and screams, "I'm going to make you a star." Your job is to go out and do the very best you can. Don't worry about changing the lives of the judges. Think about changing your own.

Singing From the Opera

In many cases, people insist that when you audition for a specific opera, you sing arias from the opera. I have heard singers complain about this, that the director and conductor have no imaginations, that the arias aren't ready, and why should the singer put him or herself in a position of singing something not ready? It's true that this can be a problem; I know all the arguments. But the fact of the matter is, the people auditioning you want to hear something from the opera they're doing. They need a basis for comparison, for one thing. For another, it just makes sense.

You may find yourself singing for a young theater director who doesn't have sufficient experience to be able to say, Well, she's singing Gilda, but I really think she can do *Il Barbiere di Siviglia*. If you can't for some reason sing the exact piece, you've got to get close. Or even better, learn the music. But do not, under any circumstance, sing anything that is below your standard for preparation.

Once you get into the habit of learning a piece of music well, it is not such an overwhelming task. If your technique is solid, and your learning technique itself is solid, you know where to start: with the words, with the music. And when it's time to put the two together, you know which vocal problems to solve before you start singing it, how to get your imagination involved. Remind yourself of the stylistic goals. What is French music style like? Oh, yes, this is the music where I really have to sing lightly on the "schwa" vowels. This is Mozart; that means I can't pound the top notes. You have all of your assets as you start.

Another thing you can do is to go to a very experienced coach and say, "Tell me all about this piece of music, show me how it goes, show me how to learn it. Tell me the traditions and pitfalls." And if your technique permits you to do that, let them show you the difficulties and the solutions. Some singers work best alone, but it doesn't hurt to give yourself the benefit of all the coaching you can.

There's a wonderful phrase called "in preparation." Use it if the opportunity calls for it. "This aria is in preparation. If you would like to hear it, I will sing one aria which I use often for auditions, and I will sing this aria from the opera for you which is in preparation." I would never, never advise you to sing an aria that you had not planned to sing, one which was not immediately in your mind, without that caveat. Even at that, be sure that it's not possible to come back and sing the aria another day.

If you are auditioning for a certain job and you are comfortable beginning with an aria from that opera, do so. If you are comfortable with something else, your introduction has to be very carefully planned. When they're doing *Rigoletto* and you want to start with *La Bohème*: "I would like to start with 'Che gelida manina.' I also have 'Questa o quella' with me."

Glitches in the Process

All that out of the way, if you're well-prepared, the rest should go like clockwork. Except that sometimes it doesn't. So now let's go through what can throw you for a loop, no matter how often you've rehearsed.

I've gone to several auditions as an accompanist where normally the singer has the right to sing the first piece. But the opera director didn't want to hear the chosen piece; he had limited time and needed to hear something else. The singer and I were both totally taken by surprise. We weren't prepared to be flexible — a grave mistake. Yes, we were prepared to do the second piece after the first, but we should have had in the back of our minds that we might have to switch. Never assume.

A singer may also discount the auditioners' intelligence and write the whole audition off because of a hole in someone's knowledge. Once I was playing auditions for an opera company, and a baritone announced, "I will sing 'Per me giunto' and 'O Carlo, ascolta'," naming both parts of the aria from *Don Carlo*. As I began to play, I heard one of the music directors say, "One aria by one composer is all that's required, please." Well, it *was* one aria by one composer. You must never assume auditioner ignorance, indications to the contrary. Particularly in a competition, you may be auditioning for another singer, a tenor, perhaps, who really doesn't know the soprano repertoire. Or the judge is a soprano who doesn't know every in and out of the bass repertoire. It doesn't mean that they can't distinguish bad voices from good or good performances from bad. It just means they don't know that aria. If that kind of incorrect information materializes, give them the best you have anyway.

There are rare occasions when an audition needs to be stopped. Obviously, if the pianist starts in the wrong key or plays the wrong notes so you are unable to get your first note, you can't very well continue. And this has happened. But there's a way to handle it in a pleasant, relaxed way and in good spirit. If your accompanist has taken off in an impossible tempo, and during the course of your singing, you have been unable to speed him up or slow him down (without, of course, waving your hands), then you're going to have to stop. But don't stamp your foot and glare at the accompanist. If you do this, don't bother to continue singing, because you will have created a poor impression with the listeners (especially if it's their accompanist). Demonstrate with your pianist that you are capable of cooperation, kindness and professionalism.

I have a question for all of us who perform. Why do we comment on a mistake in public? Let's say you run out of breath. Let's not announce it to the entire room. It just isn't professional. It happens, but *never comment on your work while you're doing it*. If you make a mistake, try — try with all your concentration — not to show it on your face or announce it. It's not necessary. The mistake won't kill you in most cases, but the indication of it just might.

Also, don't do things like stand *en pointe* while going for a high D. It's physiologically unsound and looks like bad, even if you have nice legs. This is where outside observation before beginning the audition process is important. But you would be surprised how often that type of thing is seen in an audition.

Offenses, Perceived and Otherwise

People do eat sandwiches while you're singing, and they do talk to each other, at times not in a whisper. It may seem as if they're not listening. If you're paying attention to what they're doing, you're not paying attention to what you're doing. You have to disengage from them and perform for them. You perform for the audience — you feel a connection with the audience. The man who's asleep in the first row shouldn't distract you. He may challenge you, but rather than despairing, you have to rise to the challenge. And if nothing else, it's another audition under your belt, and that certainly can't hurt the next one.

If you are extraordinarily offended, if you feel something so terribly destructive is happening during your aria that you cannot go on, you may want to stop. But you take the chance that you'll not be invited back soon. If you truly don't want to continue, you have to do the same as you would if you were hired for a production and you found you had misjudged the situation — expect not to come back. If you feel this is more than you can ever tolerate, then you have to leave. You have to decide for yourself what you believe in, how much you want a certain job, how much you want to sing under very difficult circumstances.

Someone I know, now out of the business, but very talented,

traveled into a city to do her third audition for a large opera company. For her second audition, she was told she would be singing for the head of the company. However, when she arrived for that audition, the head of the opera company did not appear. At the third audition, when she was again told she would be unable to sing for the this person, the singer threw a complete temper tantrum and stormed off the stage. As I said, she's now out of the business.

Her upset, her disappointment were understandable. What should she have done? In her case, exactly what she did. She did not have the temperament for the opera business and is now very happily uninvolved in it. You have to keep your eye on what you're doing. The opera director may have been called away that day. Students of mine have gone to sing for some well-known conductors, only to find their auditions canceled because of last-minute schedule conflicts. This is as disappointing for coaches and teachers as it is for singers, but it's not the end of the world. There will be another opportunity.

Perhaps a better approach, rather than ranting and raving at the auditioners, would be to follow the advice of a friend's mother to her singer-daughter: "Keep your throat open and your mouth shut."

Another singer I know did his long-awaited stage audition for a major opera company, and as he stood there singing, an emergency occurred which required the scheduled opera to be changed for that evening. So you know that they really didn't listen to him very carefully. He said afterward, "No, I've done all the auditioning I'm going to for those people. I won't sing for them again." That's unfortunate. But it was his decision, and in his case, pride came before his desire to work for that company.

All of these decisions that you make are part of the practice of being in the business. These are individual decisions with no right or wrong answers. Perhaps you are hired to do *Don Pasquale*. You envision a normal production. You arrive at the theater, and it's a modern production. You have to run up and down the stairs and do things you never even remotely thought possible, let alone desirable. And you have to decide, Am I going to stay there and do it with all my heart, or am I going to go home? And if you can't find a way to believe in what you're doing, you must forfeit the job. Enormous flexibility goes into being a musician, and sometimes, depending on where you are in your career or where you want to be, you may have to reorganize your temperament and your opinions. Maybe some personal pride has to be exchanged for pride in your performance. Maybe some of your ego has to be exchanged for the success of the production. Learn to look at it from another point of view.

Other than emphasizing preparation, what's the best, the very best advice I can give a singer to help prepare for an audition? Sit in on one yourself, if at all possible. Being on the other side of the stage will tell you more than all the advice in the world.

%   %   %

Chapter Eleven

Your New Role:
Working Professional

When I first started in opera, I thought that all singers kept coaching and studying forever. It was a big shock when I saw what happened to certain singers with the onset of the pressure of regular performing, the necessity for stability during performing, and the inability to destabilize long enough to learn something new. Learning means change, and performing is very difficult when making big changes, or even small ones. It's also scary, so new information doesn't want to enter the psyche. Information about a new way to breathe becomes risky to incorporate when you're out there singing. We like to hang on to what we have: this chair is comfortable, because I know this chair.

Have a smart sense of caution, but also a spirit of adventure. Change can be thrilling. If the voice were to stay just where you put it, that would be one thing, but for the most part, it doesn't. With every opportunity to sing, the voice learns more things, some of which are good and should be kept, and others which should be discarded.

The voice and the body do not stay the same — not for singers, not for athletes, not for dancers. Retraining and advancing in the training are essential. Richard Tucker told me one of the most important things I have learned. You have to get better, or you get worse. There's no in-between. The realization that your voice can be seriously harmed is something that most young singers don't have. But it really can happen. Great careers have been lost by careless handling of a great instrument. Sacrifice is truly necessary, and most of us would be willing to make the great sacrifice. But the small sacrifices we must make every day — No, I can't drink red wine because I have to sing, No, I have to go to bed early, I can't join the party — these are harder to make. And the discipline with which you use your voice is not a free gift. You must not demand instant gratification from your voice. You have to nurture it and bring it to people who can polish and love it and keep it from going astray. View it as a child, if you will, whose growth possibilities are almost endless, for good and for bad. When the voice gets to be an adult, then you can trust it a little more — but only when it's a real adult, a mature adult.

Your perceptions of music have to deepen. Each time you work with a great conductor, you add to yourself. But in order for that to be incorporated, the earth has to be turned over, and the new richness has to be added into your being and new thought generated from that.

Continued Training

The way the opera business works often makes continued study and training difficult at best. There are the engagements way in advance, the financial responsibilities that may cause a singer to take more engagements than he should, as well as the excitement of constant new artistic and financial opportunities.

Above all, there are the musical opportunities. Are you going to turn down a singing engagement with Mehta, a recording with Levine? Turn down a chance to work with Kleiber? Are you going to refuse your European debut with, "No, this is the month I reserved to study?"

A singer is often so anxious to get a career off the ground one way or the other, that once he or she is "there," the desire to take advantage of every performing opportunity that comes along is almost overwhelming. The temptation is incredible. If you don't think long-term, it boils down to, "I've got to learn this role," as opposed to, "I need to study and absorb this new role." And the role, instead of yielding new discoveries about your voice, your performing abilities, your perceptive abilities, your creative abilities, just draws on what's there. So nothing new is created, including what you do with your voice. And any small, unhealthy tendency is not heard early enough by the people who know your voice well to be detected in time. It will have to become a major problem for somebody to hear it. By that time, you've got to stop completely in order to correct it.

Singers who are just beginning, I've noticed, coach a lot. It's almost as if it's their only avenue for performing. Also, to break into the field of opera, there's almost no other way but to coach. Then, as soon as the career begins to accelerate a little bit — Violetta this month, Mimi next, Micaela the third — the time for coaching seems to diminish in proportion to how much work the singer has. That time for exacting and careful preparation becomes less and less. In some ways, that's okay, because hopefully the singer has acquired learning skills, can analyze an opera more quickly, and is more proficient in languages. Naturally, when you're on your sixth Verdi opera, it takes a little less time than your first Verdi opera. Still, a reasonable amount of time is required for a body to absorb, not only the vocal skills, but also the style, body language and understanding of a character.

One of the ways to give yourself that time is to have the invincible courage of your convictions and schedule learning time into your work schedule. Make a date with yourself to study. This still has to be fairly flexible, because unfortunately, the most important jobs of your career will keep coming along when you were supposed to study. As a result, "Her singing in the new production of *Mefistofele* was not bad. Let's see her do Musetta next month." "Well, a lot of potential." Six months of a lot of potential, and you no longer have any. You're the promising young prize fighter who never wins a big match.

A golf pro thinks nothing of finding a particular coach to help with the placement of a thumb and another coach for swing. He draws on an assortment of videos and books which utilize techniques from Bobby Jones to Jack Nicklaus — and nobody laughs. The ice skater has coaches, weight-lifting instructors, dance teachers, choreographers, sports psychologists, nutritionists, costumers. Nobody thinks a thing of it. When we get to sports, somehow it goes with the territory. Was there ever a baseball team without spring training? Somehow, we only allow for the training period of singers before they've started their careers. But they desperately need it all during their careers. Recordings, television performances that are released as videos — all these things are so permanent now, that the idea of doing a performance which only remains in some people's memories is becoming an oddity. Not only that, there is a responsibility to the people who learn from these tapes and discs, as you once did.

The business will wait for you to realize your potential, but not forever. The smart singers really prepare. Artists like Renata Scotto, Alfredo Kraus, Mirella Freni and Luciano Pavarotti spend not only large amounts of time in preparation, but in choosing a season's roles. And they never stop studying, refinding those roles, both vocally and emotionally. Know what you can do. And hard as it is, I don't think that there's anybody in the world who simply will not respect, "I'm sorry, I need to study during that period." If you have to switch your study period, switch it. But don't take it away. You think you can't miss an opportunity, but in the long run, the opportunity will catch up with you. If singers of large experience need study time, why don't you?

One of the excuses I hear is, "Well, I really can't afford to coach." If it takes 20 session at $60 a session, that's a cost of $1,200. If your performance fee is only $1,000, you're going in debt for $200. Yes. But again, singers, think of the big picture. You will have the role in really good shape. The next time you do this role for $1,500, you'll probably need a $600 investment. The third time, for $2,000, you'll only need a $500 investment. You won't have to pay $3,000 years later to relearn the role and correct the mistakes. The ease and wealth of detail you acquire in the beginning make the work worth the time and money. Even monetarily, preparation makes sense.

And everything is negotiable in this world. I've had so many cases of coaching somebody in a role and being paid when they were paid. All of us want the singer out on the stage. That's where everything is happening. We don't want to keep them in the studio. On the other hand, investing in a role that you learn badly, perform at less than your best, is as costly an investment as I know. It's like a dry oil well. Everything is costly when you have to do it over and over again.

You need the strongest and best preparation and re-preparation. Just because you did a role that way last month doesn't mean you should do it again that way. Switch the tires. Oil the machine. Don't sing a role six years later the way you did it the first time. Become more profound, more subtle, sing it better. That's the way to grow in this business.

Good Coaching

From the singers I've worked with, I've seen that it can be very helpful to have several coaches of long standing who are completely familiar with your style of studying, your style of singing. You should have, if possible, one on each continent. People you trust, to whom you can go in all conditions and ask honest questions, and who have good ears. People who will come and listen to the performance, note passages that are perhaps out of tune, out of line, of lesser quality, and act as minder of the store while you are on stage. Then you can afford to take suitable risk, make suitable growth, suitable progress, and have someone on your team monitoring you.

Another reason for having more than one coach is that some coaches specialize in specific repertoire, and you may want to go to one for a particular role. Some are particularly expert in one language, others are known for an exceptionally fine-tuned ear. A coach who is a conductor can give you something different from the coach who is a composer. There are coaches who are fabulous with voices — vocal line, pitches — without being voice teachers. Some coaches are particularly tuned in to the drama, some are particularly good at helping polish a piece, some are especially proficient at helping you break into a piece.

We know the danger of doing roles that are too heavy, but I wonder if there is not the same or greater danger in singing a role not grooved into the body, one that the throat, the body, the breathing are always groping for. How do I distribute the top of the voice? How do I go through the passagio?

There well may be a singer who deals well with problems by ignoring them, and if you have a natural capacity to work that way, that's fine. However, it's no use pretending a problem doesn't exist if you're the kind of singer who needs to address it. Singing is a little bit like measles; there's no textbook case. That's one of the reasons a coach becomes so important, particularly a kind of central coach you can keep going back to, who knows your voice and will hear if you're beginning to sing too heavily in the middle, if the top is beginning to spread. Suddenly, you're carrying your chest voice up very high. Didn't you used to have a high C?

The coach who's on a power trip, however, is one to be avoided. Fortunately, most people in this business are in it because they love it, but it would be unrealistic to think that everybody can maintain high ideals all the time. There's the factor of being human. If you come across a teacher or coach whose need to control you as a singer is more important than the desire to reveal your talents, it's a good time to go. There are singers who need to be controlled, who need the iron fist. But for the most part, you must consider the respect due you as an artist, the respect due your opinion, the respect due your feelings about your voice, yourself, your career, whether from manager, voice teacher or coach. When you find yourself in a milieu where your opinions and questions are not respected, where there is no interaction, but only dictation, consider if that fulfills your present needs or frustrates them.

Most of the time, your central figure — whether voice teacher, wife, husband or coach — is vital. But resist the temptation to be with somebody who only speaks about your faults or who only speaks about your perfection. There is a time, when a singer is beginning to develop a unique artistic and emotional personality, that he or she doesn't want to hear anything from anyone but their mentor. The first person who disagrees with them is tossed out of their lives. Well, you don't have to do what other people say, but it's often wise to consider it.

On the other hand, to choose a coach who abuses you regularly just so you can continue to feel bad about yourself is not advisable. Wait for the reviewers for that. I've seen people caught up in the web of attempting to prove something to a coach instead of developing their best abilities. Supportive, smart, knowledgeable and available people are what you want.

Before you begin the opera, it's beneficial to find somebody who has performed the opera a hundred times, who has coached it with six people. Have them take you through the opera: Here are the difficult words, This pitch is often wrong, Here you need to pace it like this. Ask them to give you an overview, a translation, a feeling for what the whole piece is about. Talk to them about it, discuss all the various possibilities — not "This is the way it's got to be," but "This is the way Serafin did it or Levine did it. This used to be cut; it's not always cut now. The appoggiaturas are thus. Here's the page where there's no room for breath — tank up."

Learn all the possibilities about the piece. Talk about the role with the singers you know who have sung it. Play it through on the piano or ask someone to play it for you. Sing it an octave lower, perhaps. And when you've done all that, then I think it's a good time to start applying the voice — but not before. You don't want to use a very expensive voice to start cold; much better to find out what those notes are all about first. Not everyone is the same and reacts, thinks or studies in the same way, but it's great to begin where a fine artist has left off and take advantage of their sage advice. He might say, "No, it's not easy to sing *La Bohème* and the tenor in *Der Rosenkavalier* at the same time." But, "Yes, you can sing *I Puritani* and *Semiramide* at the same time. These are fine together for the tenor."

There are a few singers who do their break-in work completely by themselves, others who like to work with their coach from the moment they open the score. Approaching a new role encompasses many different feelings: excitement, nervousness, anticipation, anxiety. Taking the road that gets you over those bumps best is important.

When you go to the production itself, there are people who

set up the rules. Some opera houses are tight organizations and not explorative with works. But they're all striving to elicit the best art out of a singer that they can, and the best performance. If you're coaching the opera with a coach who is not involved in the production, you have to make the coach aware of the specific circumstances. "I have to run up a flight of stairs during this, hold this note here, this is slower." The other alternative is to coach solely with the people involved in the opera.

Dealing with Difficult Situations

In your performing career, you will meet great conductors and stage directors. They are never a problem. However, you will also encounter inexperienced conductors and directors; that can be a more difficult. Sometimes, a conductor or stage director will do something just because they lack the ability to do anything else. He's doing a pick-up with a long note because he can't quite get his arm down, or she is staging it one way because she simply hasn't the experience to think of another way. Find out whether you can talk to them, how capable or willing they are to do something other than what they have just told you they want. Find a straightforward way, with tact and modesty, without antagonism and with sincere interest, to reach a negotiated solution. "Negotiated" means you don't get everything you want.

As a young singer, you're often not sure what you want anyway, and if you are a very experienced singer, it sometimes means you want to do it the way you just did it. It also sometimes means that you know exactly how you have to have it, and any other way won't do, because your voice just won't negotiate it any other way.

I think every singer has certain points like that in an aria, an opera. Hone your communication skills (college is a place to practice). Go home and consider that, No, I didn't get these three points I really need, let alone the three points that I want. I succeeded only in making this person angry. Now, how can I redo this so that I can convey what I want and need?

There are some singers with the magic touch who can say, "Maestro, what do you think about . . ." with such enthusiasm, who can come up with an idea so catching that the maestro, in spite of himself, is brought into it. Or to the stage director: "You know, maybe if I tried it like this? How would that look?" These singers have a way of inspiring others, so that everyone truly begins to work as a unit.

Defensiveness seems to be one of the biggest problems. But singers are often defensive because they need to be. "No, no, I can't do that" is often a realistic statement! When you see that you have to run down the stairs while singing the high E flat, it's often not a bad idea to allow yourself the privilege of failing at it. That way, everybody can see that you're not just being a pain in the neck — this simply doesn't work in your body. Maybe for the last soprano who did it, it was okay, but you can offer other things. I think here the approach is again negotiability and the kind of careful, non-neurotic thinking process that allows you to see a way to solve a problem without developing a sense of "He's out to get me." The ability to understand and indicate what tempi you need accompanies the knowledge that you, in turn, must support a conductor when he needs your attention, when your dragging the beat the slightest bit, for instance, is going to ruin his preparation for a tempo change. The same is true of the stage director. No matter what quibbles you may have about certain sections, give him what he must have. Directors and conductors have made huge investments of thought and time in musical and dramatic decisions. Your inability to remember to stand on that corner as opposed to this corner means that the chorus is going to have a problem when they enter, so you must follow directions.

There are things that are absolute givens, because too much depends on them. And those are places which are generally not negotiable. If you do those things for a conductor or a stage director, then find the points that are negotiable, you can generally work things out.

You do find half the time that the stage director or conductor lifts you beyond yourself. The other half of the time, it's work. And there is the costume designer who had a tall, bosomless woman in mind, or a tall, slender man, and here you are. There's the director who had a blond wig in mind for you when it's the last thing you need. The more informed you are about who you are and who you're working with before you go into rehearsal, the better off you are. On your first few jobs, you may say, "I'll take it. I don't care." But there's only a certain price you can pay, and if the end cost is going to be that you look ridiculous and cannot possibly sound good, maybe this isn't the job for you. Sometimes, young singers who get a start in seemingly inappropriate places, like big opera companies, can have a better time of it, because they are dealing with people who are more experienced, people who are used to dealing with singers who have different needs and who understand that, Yes, we have to move the chair, because your legs aren't as long as so-and-so's, and you can't cover the same amount of ground. Maybe the spitcurls on the side are not becoming for you.

Learning to say "no" is very important. But know how and when to use that skill. "I can't rehearse six more hours. I can't accept this role. I can't sing this tessitura consistently." Obviously, saying "no" becomes easier the bigger your reputation. But at all costs, take care of yourself.

Professional Life and Behavior

Communication is important, and not only in English. A three or four hundred word fluency in each language is nice, enough to say, "Where is the stage door, please?" "Maestro, that's really too fast." "Yes, stage director, I would very much like to do it like this." "Where is the ladies' room, office, men's room, telephone?" "My room is too hot." Learn the important phrases. Not only because you will probably be having a career in all these countries, but more importantly, because you will be dealing with directors, conductors and fellow singers of other nationalities. It would be nice to be able to say "Good morning" to them. "How are you?" "I enjoyed the rehearsal." "I have a problem with this."

When you sing professionally, you get the exalted days when everything is working, but that doesn't happen every day. When you have to sing every day, some days are just not as good as others. But what being a professional singer means is that you can make it work when it doesn't work. Anybody can be an inspired teacher for five minutes. Being a teacher means that when you feel like you haven't got a thought in your head, you can dig one up. And that's the most important thing — to be able to produce a consistent performance. It's not what you are feeling that counts, it's what you can make the audience feel. So what if you're not "on" that particular night. That doesn't mean you can't convince your audience.

Every few years, I go out and buy a new score, for instance, when I'm starting my tenth production of *La Traviata*, and start it all over again. I restudy *La Bohème* every couple of years from an entirely different point of view. If I don't, the piece isn't fresh for me as a coach, let alone for the singer who winds up doing so many performances. Then we settle down into the two most blasphemous words in this business: predictable and routine. Predictable and routine to perform, and predictable and routine to hear.

Pay attention to basic human behavior and courtesy. Don't count yourself out before you open your mouth to sing. Act with consideration for all the people who help you along the way. Very often, secretaries and administrative assistants are trusted employees whose opinions are valued. All it takes is, "He's a real neurotic," or "She screamed at me on the telephone," or "He's so easy to work with," and you may find yourself in or out of the running. Managers, opera directors and coaches want people with whom they can work. We respond to those who touch us, whether we're singing or talking. Remember the human element in this business.

Have an understanding of the pressures people are under. Of course, your career and your voice are your number one priority. But do you honestly believe you're the only person calling for an audition appointment, requesting a coaching? If your first, second, third and fourth calls are not responded to, if you've left a hundred messages on an answering machine and no one has gotten back to you, don't decide you're hated. Keep calling, or write. Don't take it personally. People are busy! Phone tag is a way of life. People in the opera world tend to have many tugs on them and very crowded schedules which often involve travel. No one wants to be talking on the phone. We all want to be doing music. You're not alone.

Always, always, always carry an extra picture and résumé with you. If you have management, your manager, believe it or not, may not have sent your materials. Or your materials may have gotten lost. If the company is from out of town, certain things may have been left behind. If the judges do not have a picture and résumé, in most cases, the audition is over then and there. When they are discussing the singers at the end of the day, you will be left out.

Also, be sure you have a professional-looking picture and résumé. Get good advice on them and the rest of your materials. They represent you when you are not there to represent yourself. Have your résumé typeset, and go to a professional photographer. Don't have your photos taken by your brother-in-law who has a camera or by the local portrait photographer, unless they know the particular requirements of a theatrical picture.

Have a good knowledge of the inner workings of our business. Managers and coaches can often help you with this information process, and there are many good master classes. Many theaters will hear a singer and have no place to put them, because everything is booked two or three years in advance. This is a problem with opera, especially in the United States. Engagements are booked so far in the future that when new talent comes along, debuts are often delayed for years. This is done because, if that house doesn't hire you, another will. You can do a perfectly wonderful audition, and nothing will happen for two or three years. Then, when a cancellation occurs, you get a call. An audition that has no immediate outcome is not necessarily a bad audition, unless you're talking about a place that's hiring people next week. But for big theaters, when you give them a good repertoire list, they have something they can look at for several years to come, and know where to look if they need your particular voice type.

If you find your career isn't bringing you what you'd hoped, realize that nothing you've learned — the discipline, the self-motivation, the study techniques, the communication skills — will ever leave you. They will stand you in good stead whether you continue in a music-related field or move on to something else. Never negate your training or your love of music. We all know that music is a demanding master, and a long career in it may not be to every taste, talent or temperament. There are other avenues in music to pursue besides singing: administration, teaching, music therapy, writing, criticism, music publishing. If the only thing that will make you happy is singing at the Met, then you are probably not in the singing profession for the right reasons. Perhaps you can find why you need that applause and get it more easily someplace else. If you're singing because it makes you happy, and you want to be the very best singer you can possibly be, stay in and be grateful for whatever opportunities come your way to practice your craft. Also, remember this — just because you've stopped being a *professional* singer doesn't mean you have to stop singing. There are churches, hospitals, community theaters that might welcome your beautiful voice and expertise.

If you have something else that you really love that makes you feel fulfilled, then do it. Only if you are the kind of person whose life will never be complete unless you have a singing career should you stay the course. It's easier and less costly to become a brain surgeon. But "singing career" can be defined in many ways. Look into the advantages of being a big fish in a small pond. You might find you're much happier.

Also, you don't have to be an opera "star." There are lots and lots of ways to have a very satisfying life in opera. Some people like a settled life. They like a steady cash flow and don't want to be bothered with airplanes, motel rooms, publicity and crazy schedules. You can have security and still be in opera. The Metropolitan Opera Chorus is fabulous. We have many people who do the very necessary small roles, and it means you can stay in a theater and have a kind of home life. There are other big theaters in the United States and in Europe that afford these kinds of opportunities.

Whatever you do, don't forget to take care of yourself. We realize you have to chase around the world today, but giving yourself the best living conditions possible is important, even if it's only really possible when you're in the upper price range. Do the best you can at $500 a performance. If you're sick or depressed, you won't be able to sing well.

Have a laryngologist who knows what your vocal chords look like when they are healthy, so that you can recognize problems that indicate that you shouldn't sing. One performance can cause serious damage to unhealthy vocal chords. On the other hand, you don't want to cancel a performance if it's fine for you to sing.

I urge you, most of all, to enjoy the process. Enjoy the studying, the growing and the achievement. Be the best colleague in the world and the most heart-warming person. Bring sunshine, high spirits, energy and thoughtfulness into the rehearsal process. Opera companies enjoy singers who are satisfied with the accommodations, the rehearsal place, the director, who work hard, don't catch cold and don't have dyspepsia. Don't be seduced by the media of the past into believing that the temperamental diva route is the way to go. This type of myth has grown up because we like glamour and are fascinated by people who have a great deal of emotional electricity. Bring glamour, temperament and emotional electricity to the stage, not the rehearsal hall. Rehearsal schedules are difficult. The person who bends over backwards to be cooperative and helpful, who says, Yes, I can, more than, No, I don't want to, are appreciated and more than loved.

If you find that you're only hired once by places and then never again, check into why. If you make a mistake in your relationship with somebody, it can be remedied. Talk frankly and honestly, and listen openly.

I have so much cherished the experience of being on tour with a great company like the Metropolitan Opera and witnessing the marvelous interaction that can exist between singers. It does take a little while to get there, but early in your career is often the time when you can begin to practice the kind of self-control, generosity and all of the factors that are brought out by different, and generally more highly energized personalities.

I had a good piece of advice the first day I went to the Met. "Stand outside the door, calm down, realize again you're very lucky to be doing this job, and how all the minor aggravations are really only that. And go in smiling." It sounds easy enough, and it is easy enough. That's why I wonder why more people don't do it, and why I hear on the phone, "Yes, Joan, we tried out that singer, but she was so difficult to work with. I'm not sure we ever want her back. Yes, and such-and-such a company did call, and we did give them that report about her, so I don't think they want her either." For this to happen after all the work, all the technique, the studying, the language, everything else that's gone into this career, seems to me a great pity.

Don't indulge in the tearing down of other people, but build up the cast in which you will be one superb part. The better your cast, the better you are. This is a truth. The more one singer gets excited and feeds another, the better the performances you all give, the kind that "clicks." There is no way to push the others back and shine yourself.

The ability to recreate, to be spontaneous with a piece of music that you have thought out, worked on, slaved over — the ability to believe in the total magic of something that you have analyzed, dissected and put back together — these are only a few of the thrilling challenges that face you as a singer. To learn how to develop an instrument that you can't see and the satisfaction that it brings is something that should be cherished. As Stanislavski said in his book, *Stanislavski on Opera*, "Search for artistry within yourselves. Keep alive the muscles of creativity. Above all, proceed with logic and plant yourself firmly on that. The composer gives us everything: the rhythm for the feeling, intonation for each word, and a melody which patterns the emotions." We must find a true basis for the wisdom given us in such words and make it our own. Maybe this is the best way to consider what our lifetime attempt — and it is a lifetime attempt — at being completely prepared is all about. It's the most fascinating voyage in the world!

In bocca al lupo.

✄   ✄   ✄

Suggested Reading

Ardoin, John. *Callas at Juilliard: The Master Classes*. Alfred A. Knopf.

Ashbrook, William. *Donizetti and His Operas*. Cambridge University Press.

Ashbrook, William. *The Operas of Puccini*. Oxford University Press.

Bawtree, Michael. *The New Singing Theatre*. Oxford University Press.

Budden, Julian. *The Operas of Verdi, Volume 1*. Praeger.

Budden, Julian. *The Operas of Verdi, Volume 2*. Oxford University Press.

Cassell's French Dictionary. MacMillan Publishing.

Cassell's German Dictionary. MacMillan Publishing.

Cassell's Italian Dictionary. MacMillan Publishing.

Colorni, Evelina. *Singers' Italian: A Manual of Diction and Phonetics*. Schirmer.

Craig, David. *The Art of Singing Onstage*. Schirmer Books.

Davenport, Marcia. *Mozart.* Charles Scribner Publishers.

Davenport, Marcia. *Of Lena Geyer.* Charles Scribner Publishers.

Fischer-Dieskau, Dietrich. *The Fischer-Dieskau Book of Lieder.* Alfred A. Knopf.

Gallwey, W. Timothy. *The Inner Game of Tennis.* Bantam Books.

Geertz, Clifford. *The Interpretation of Cultures.* Basic Books (Harper/Colophon Books).

Goldovsky, Boris. *Bringing Soprano Arias to Life.* Scarecrow Press.

Grant, Donald Jay. *A Short History of Opera.* Columbia University Press.

Grubb, Thomas. *Singing in French: A Manual of French Diction and French Vocal Repertoire.* Schirmer Books.

Grun, Bernard. *Timetables of History*, based upon Werner Stein's *Kulturfahrplan.* Simon & Schuster.

Hines, Jerome. *Great Singers on Singing.* Limelight Editions.

Kagen, Sergius. *Music for the Voice.* Indiana University Press.

Mann, William. *The Operas of Mozart.* Oxford University Press.

Marshall, Madeleine. *The Singer's Manual of English Diction.* Schirmer Books.

Miller, Philip L. *The Ring of Words, an Anthology of Song Texts.* Anchor Books (Doubleday & Co.).

Miller, Stuart. *Understanding Europeans.* John Muir Publications.

Osbourne, Charles. *The Complete Operas of Verdi.* Alfred A. Knopf.

Owens, Richard. *The Professional Singer's Guide to New York.* American Institute of Musical Studies.

Papolos, Janet. *The Performing Artists Handbook.* Writers Digest Books.

Ristad, Eloise. *Soprano on Her Head: Right-Side-Up Reflection on Life — & Other Performances*. Real People.

Robinson, Paul. *Opera and Ideas*. Harper and Row.

Schmidgall, Gary. *Shakespeare and Opera*. Oxford University Press.

Siebs Deutsche Aussprache German Pronunciation Dictionary. Walter De Gruyter and Co., Berlin.

Stanislavski, Constantin, and Rumayntsev, Pavel. *Stanislavski on Opera*. Theatre Arts Books.

Summers-Dossena, Ann. *Getting It All Together: A Handbook for Performing Artists in Classical Music and Ballet*. Excalibur Publishing.

Uris, Dorothy. *To Sing in English: A Guide to Improved Diction*. Boosey & Hawkes.

Weaver, William. *The Golden Century of Italian Opera from Rossini to Puccini*. Thames and Hudson.

Weaver, William. *Puccini: The Man and His Music*. Dutton.

Weaver, William. *Seven Puccini Librettos*. Norton.

Weaver, William. *Seven Verdi Librettos*. Norton.

Weisstein, Ulrich. *The Essence of Opera*. Norton.

Zingarelli Vocabulario della Lingua Italiana. Nichola Zanichelli SpA, Bologna.

Index

About the Authors

Joan Dornemann is one of the most highly respected opera coaches in the world today. In her position as Assistant Conductor of the Metropolitan Opera, she prepares the most prominent international artists for their performances at the Met. These prestigious artists have included Luciano Pavarotti, Placido Domingo, Mirella Freni, Jose Carreras, Sherrill Milnes, Kiri Te Kanawa, Renata Scotto, Marilyn Horne, Alfredo Kraus and Montserrat Caballe. In addition, Ms. Dornemann has prompted under the batons of James Levine, James Conlon, Michelangelo Veltri and Carlos Kleiber. It was Montserrat Caballe who interested Ms. Dornemann in her first prompting assignment: the Gran Liceo in Barcelona. That quickly led to engagements in Trieste, the Spoleto Festival, the New York City Opera and, in 1974, the Met. A great supporter of young singers, she is director of the Israel Vocal Arts Institute and teaches master classes throughout the United States, as well as in Israel, New Zealand, Canada and Puerto Rico. Ms. Dornemann received an Emmy Award for her collaboration in the highly acclaimed *Live from the Met* first telecast of *La Bohème* with Luciano Pavarotti and Renata Scotto, has been featured in *People* magazine, appeared on *The Tonight Show*, and was the subject of a segment on *Sunday Morning* with Charles Kuralt.

Maria Ciaccia is a former student of Joan Dornemann's who has appeared internationally in opera, musical comedy, television and cabaret. She is the author of *Bloomin', A Novel in Three Acts*, as well as a contributing editor to *Hollywood Studio Magazine*. Her upcoming books include *Dreamboats: Hollywood Hunks of the '50s* and *Casta Diva, An Operatic Novel*.